# MANAGING RENTAL PROPERTIES LIKE A PRO

### Susan J. Underhill
### with Ken Upshaw

**PROBUS PUBLISHING COMPANY**
Chicago, Illinois
Cambridge, England

This publication is designed to provide accurate and authoritative information in regard to the subject matter covered. It is sold with the understanding that the publisher is not engaged in rendering legal, accounting or other professional service.

ISBN 1-55738-250-6

Printed in the United States of America

IPC

1  2  3  4  5  6  7  8  9  0

It is impossible to achieve success in isolation. My journey has been made possible with the help and guidance of many people. To those who have helped me (you know who you are) I extend my heartfelt thanks.

# Contents

# Preface

# After You Buy It, You Have to Manage It

**N**ow that you own a rental property, how will you manage it? Many owners, concerned about a lack of time or their own lack of knowledge, elect to hire a professional management company to do the job for them. Others, however, prefer to protect their investment by overseeing the management of the property themselves.

Most real estate investment books overlook entirely the problem of managing a property once you have acquired it, utterly dismissing this critical part of an investment strategy. Other "experts" on investment strategy create the impression that successful property management is a cinch, with advice such as the following:

"An effective investment strategy is to purchase a building that has been poorly managed and therefore can be bought below market price. After a period of good management, which raises the value of the property, the building can be resold with an excellent profit."

Such advice assumes that a real estate investor knows what good property management is. More than that, it assumes that the investor has the time and the skills to manage the property effectively. Neither of these is a safe assumption. Property management is not a simple task. Many long-time owners of real estate have never developed effective management strategies. Many real estate management firms do not exhibit effective management strategies.

Successful property management is a business that involves effective marketing, responsive customer service, enlightened employee relations, accurate accounting, careful quality control, and an effective collections procedure. Each component of property management is essential to the successful accomplishment of two goals: To attract and hold the best possible tenants; and to maintain the highest occupancy rate possible.

Property management is not without its pitfalls and difficulties. By following the procedures outlined in the coming pages, you can manage your property on a part-time basis with a minimum of problems and headaches. Ignore the advice, however, and you may well find yourself caught in Property Manager's Hell: a Dantean world of carping tenants, bursting pipes, leaking roofs, failed refrigerators, and broken-down boilers.

# Chapter
# 1

# A Philosophy of Property Management: Learn from Marshall Field, General George Patton, Dr. B. F. Skinner, and Mother Teresa

R ight about now you're probably thinking, "Philosophy? I don't care about philosophy. And most of all I do not want to hear a bunch of philosophical platitudes that have little to do with real-world issues." Before you rush to the next chapter, stop a moment to listen. A philosophy is nothing more than a simple statement of beliefs about something. We all hold a set of beliefs that guides our behavior in most situations. That constitutes a personal philosophy. Likewise, effective property management is based on a set of beliefs: beliefs about business; beliefs about leadership; and beliefs about people: what motivates them and how they should treat one another.

Effective property management involves more than an efficient discharge of duties. Managing a property well requires the right attitude: an attitude toward the tenants, an attitude toward the building, an attitude toward employees, an attitude toward business. A healthy and effective attitude is grounded in a sound philosophy of property management.

To develop a coherent philosophy, it is helpful to look to successful individuals to obtain clues to their success. Our philosophy of property management derives from four individuals from four completely different walks of life: General George Patton, who became a legend in World War II, Marshall Field I, who founded an extremely successful chain of department stores, Dr. B. F. Skinner, who changed the way the world looks at human behavior, and Mother Teresa, who has made a legend of herself in the streets of Calcutta.

## A Successful Philosophy of Business

Marshall Field built a retail empire in the Midwest on a simple philosophy: the customer is always right. To his employees this philosophy translated into unquestioned service for the customer, regardless of how difficult the customer might be. If the customer wanted to return an item, the item was accepted happily. If the customer wanted to spend an hour or more trying on various clothes that did not fit, that is what the customer did.

When managing a rental property, the tenants are the customers: some are a joy to work with, others are a constant pain in the neck. All tenants are looking for the same three things: they want to feel secure in their homes; they want to live in a building that is quiet, and they want to live in a clean, well-kept building. *Taking care of the customers' needs,* even when they seem unreasonable, is the basis upon which effective property management is built.

## A Philosophy of Leadership

A World War II legend, General George Patton—eccentric as he was—was successful under conditions that seemed impossible primarily because he was a general that got involved. A striking scene from the movie about his life has the general knee-deep in mud directing traffic as two columns of armored vehicles, one going East, the other North, must cross each other. Having found himself stalled in what amounted to a major traffic jam, the general—rather than yelling at the guilty parties or sending a subordinate—got into the mud himself and untangled the mess. In property management, such hands-on involvement is often the difference between a truly successful property and one that is only mediocre. Such willingness to get involved is interpreted by tenants and employees alike as *leadership*. Employees who recognize true leadership are often willing to work a little harder and a little longer and take a greater measure of responsibility than those who work for a faceless, uninvolved employer. Tenants who see that the landlord gets involved recognize that the landlord cares about what goes on around the building, and they tend to get more involved and take more responsibility for their homes.

## A Philosophy of Human Behavior

A well-known, 20th-century psychologist, Dr. B. F. Skinner pioneered the concept of behavior modification. Skinner's theory is that a behavior followed by a reward is more likely to reoccur than a behavior that is ignored. What a nice idea! If we want the tenants or employees to behave in certain ways (Paying the rent on time? Keeping the building clean?) we should reward those behaviors rather than ignore them. So instead of giving all of our attention to the tenants who are late with the rent or who cause a disturbance (although such behavior must not be ignored, either), we should reward the positive kinds of behavior that lead to a better place for everyone. We could praise a tenant for keeping his apartment nice. We could say something when we see a tenant stopping to pick up a bit of trash. A tenant who reports a problem, thus avoiding a possible catastrophe later, could receive a nice letter of appreciation. Some landlords have been known to send turkeys at Christmas. Perhaps you could give financial bonuses to tenants who consistently pay on time. With employees, try implementing various kinds of incentives. Also try praising the employee for a job well done.

The applications of Dr. Skinner's theory can be many and varied. The most important implementation, however, comes in one's everyday dealings with tenants and employees: in numerous small gestures—a wave here, a word of praise there, stopping to acknowledge a tenant's clean windows, writing a personal note to a tenant who plants a few flowers—gestures that, in their aggregate, result in a property that is easier to manage and much more successful.

## A Philosophy of Life

One would be hard-pressed to find anyone, living or dead, who more nearly embodies the philosophy of giving of one's self to help others than that of Mother Teresa. This woman, who dedicated her entire life to the poorest of the poor in Calcutta, teaches through the example of her life the beauty of loving and giving. At first glance it would seem that such a simple philosophy of love has little room in the business of property management. Because property management is a business, there is little room for giving things away. Nevertheless, dealing with present and prospective tenants and employees with the kind of caring and loving attitude embodied by Mother Teresa will, over time, prove its worth as a sound business practice.

## A Coherent Philosophy of Property Management

So there you have it: a philosophy of property management. Our belief is that successful property management strives to take care of customers' (tenants') needs, provides conspicuous, hands-on involvement, strives to reward tenants for those activities that lead to a better living environment for all, and treats tenants and employees alike in a caring and loving manner.

# Section

# I

# Successful Property Management Depends upon Effective Marketing

**T**hink of property management as a retail business. The product is the apartment; the customer is the tenant. A retail operation depends for its success upon an effective marketing strategy; so does the property management business. The only way to attract the best tenants to a building is to develop a marketing strategy and to follow it conscientiously. Marketing an apartment involves five key factors:

*Identifying the potential tenant*

Typically, a marketing strategy targets a specific type of customer. With apartment rentals, the targeted customer is the best possible tenant who would be attracted to this particular building. Defining the customer is a critical step in marketing an apartment. A campaign aimed at the wrong customer is likely to fail. The result can be either a vacant apartment or an apartment rented to an undesirable tenant.

*Establishing a price*

Setting the rent involves more than simply surveying comparable apartments. The price a person pays for an apartment is integral to their perception of quality and value. The customer you have identified will be willing to pay a particular price for your apartment. It is important to determine what that price is.

*Advertising the apartment*

Before a product can be sold, it must be introduced to the potential buyer. An effective advertising campaign will accomplish that.

*Preparing the apartment and the building for viewing*

An effective advertising campaign will attract plenty of potential customers, but the product must deliver what the ads have promised if a sale is to occur.

*Selling the apartment*

Don't expect the product to sell itself. Use a few proven sales techniques to close the deal.

# Chapter

# 2

# Identify Your Customer: Who Will Live in These Apartments?

To market an apartment, first identify who will want to live there. Each building is different and will attract a different kind of tenant. Marketing to the wrong customer makes an apartment difficult to rent, while correctly identifying the customer makes the task much easier.

To identify the customer correctly, first develop a profile of the neighborhood, then a profile of the building. Finally, develop a profile of the customer: who will be attracted to this building in this particular neighborhood?

## Profile the Neighborhood

Use a simple format to develop a profile of the neighborhood in which the building is located:

- *Housing stock:* Describe the primary type of housing available in the neighborhood: single-family, small multi-family, large multi-family, mixed, etc.

- *Density:* Is the area teeming with people and buildings or relatively uncrowded?

- *Age group:* Is the neighborhood comprised primarily of younger people, older people, a mix of ages?

- *Family status:* Is it a family neighborhood with lots of children, or are the residents primarily without children?

- *Socio-economic factors:* Are the residents of the neighborhood professionals, blue-collar workers, mixed, etc.? What is their average income?

- *Reputation:* How do people view the neighborhood? Does it have a strong ethnic identity: is it known as an Italian neighborhood, a German neighborhood, etc. Is it a changing neighborhood: is it changing for the better or for the worse? Is it a yuppie neighborhood, a slum area, a stable neighborhood, etc.

- *Safety:* Is it safe to walk the streets after dark? Is security a primary consideration?

## Profile the Building

Within the context of the neighborhood, what makes this building unique? Is it typical of the area, or are there identifiable differences?

- *Location:* Describe the immediate location of the bulding: a commercial area, residential area, a main thoroughfare, a side street, near a factory, etc.

- *Characteristics of the building:* How many units are in the building? Is it an older building? A newer building? Is it attractive? Describe the front of the building in detail. Is there a courtyard, a front yard, a backyard? Is it a high-rise, a walk-up, a single-story building?

- *Advantages that the building offers:* Describe as many advantages as possible: what will attract good tenants? Is there a good view, are there parks near-by, does the building have a pleasant yard? Is the building close to transportation, parking, shopping? Is it a quiet building? Are there modern kitchens and baths, spacious closets, hardwood floors, carpeted floors? Are the apartments spacious, comfortable, cozy?

- *Disadvantages:* Describe any characteristics that might discourage good tenants: Is the building located on a busy street, near the railroad tracks, close to commercial buildings? Does it lack amenities that most residents of the neighborhood would expect from an apartment? How many strikes does the building have against it?

## Profile the Tenant

Given the characteristics of the neighborhood and of the building, develop a realistic profile of the kind of tenant who might want to live here. Include the following characteristics:

- *Marital status*
- *Age*
- *Income*
- *Type of employment*
- *Primary mode of transportation*
- *Present living arrangement*
- *Location of present home*
- *Reason for moving*
- *Expectations for a new apartment*

There may be more than one type of potential tenant for this building. If so, describe each kind of tenant in as much detail as possible.

## Two Examples

Apartments in many buildings, because of location and other characteristics, are relatively easy to market. Others are more difficult because of one or more "strikes" against them: location, design, or other limitations. When a building is a tough sell because of inherent limiting factors, the process of analyzing and marketing to the most likely tenant is essential to the building's success.

Presented here are examples of two buildings with built-in problems, both of which were overcome by shrewd marketing. If these buildings could be filled with good tenants, there is optimism for any building, regardless of the situation.

### *Problems in "Little Italy"*

The first building (Building A) is a newer 10-unit structure located in a stable suburb on the edge of a major metropolitan city. On the light posts are signs proclaiming this the city's "Little Italy." With a reputation for some of the best Italian restaurants in the area, the neighborhood is comprised of older bungalow-type residential housing, with here and there a newer ranch or split-level home. The streets and sidewalks are for the most part clean, and many families with younger children live in the area. Here and there are sections comprised primarily of smaller apartment buildings, ranging from 6-flats to 12-flats.

While located in a desirable suburb, however, Building A has three strikes against it. It is located on a busy street, close to a busy railroad track, facing a busy parking lot. Because of the location, the previous manager encountered numerous problems leading to high vacancy rates and a series of undesirable tenants—tenants who were slow in paying the rent and who caused excessive damage to the apartments. Given the undesirable location, is it possible to attract a good tenant to this building? The previous management firm gave up trying and settled for tenants who, unfortunately, created a downward spiral. When they finally threw in the towel, vacancies in this ten-flat building stood at five, with another tenant in court for nonpayment.

**Profile of the Neighborhood:**

- *Housing stock:* Primarily single-family, with areas of small multi-family buildings. No large apartment buildings.

- *Density:* Low density.

- *Age group:* Ages are mixed, reflecting an old neighborhood whose young settle in the area to raise their own families.

- *Family status:* Many families live in the neighborhood, which offers a good supply of high-quality affordable housing.

- *Socio-economic factors:* Residents tend to be blue-collar. Average income is probably $15,000 to $30,000.

- *Reputation:* The area is a safe, stable, Italian neighborhood.

- *Safety:* Security is not a major consideration in most of the area.

**Profile of Building A:**

- *Location:*

  1. It is located on a busy street. The back of the lot is less than 30 yards from a heavily used railroad track.

  2. The front of the building faces a postal service parking lot, complete with diesel trucks idling at 5:00 A.M. The front windows open onto a maze of postal vehicles and loading docks.

  3. The back of the building is tight against another brick building, providing no view from the back windows. There is no yard.

- *Characteristics of the building:*

  1. The two-story building has 10 units, all one bedroom.

  2. The building is newer, less than 30 years old, of modern design and structure, and quite attractive.

  3. The construction is "California style," with an exposed upper and lower porch onto which each of the apartments opens.

- *Advantages:*

  1. The design is modern and attractive.

  2. The building offers off-street parking.

  3. The apartments have modern cabinet kitchens and sparkling ceramic tile baths.

  4. The apartments can be made to look modern, spacious and clean.

  5. Each apartment has central air conditioning.

  6. Each apartment has plush carpeting and glossy tile floors.

  7. The commuter train stop is just over two blocks away, providing transportation to the heart of the city.

  8. Shopping is within easy walking distance.

- *Disadvantages:*

  1. The train tracks

  2. The post office parking lot

  3. The busy street.

**Profile of a Prospective Tenant:**

Because the neighborhood offers a fine selection of single-family and multiple-family dwellings, the best prospective tenants in the area have no trouble locating top-quality apartments in desirable locations. Such tenants are not attracted to Building A because of its location. On the other hand, there are two particular types of tenants who will be attracted to this building, persons who will prove to be very desirable. The building offers a clean, modern home at an affordable rent in a desirable neighborhood. Good tenants who want that kind of apartment but cannot afford the higher rents will be drawn to this building, and there are two such types: young tenants and tenants on a fixed income.

The first kind of prospective tenant is young, single or recently married, with a good credit history but a relatively short rental history. Their earnings severely limit the amount that can be spent each month on rent. Desiring to live in a stable neighborhood but unable to afford the most desirable apartments, these prospective tenants are willing to sacrifice an ideal location for an apartment that offers two things: a clean, modern home and an affordable rent.

The Profile:

- *Marital status:* Single or recently married.
- *Age:* Young.
- *Income:* Low for the area because of inexperience on the job, but with expectations of higher pay.
- *Type of employment:* Entry level manufacturing, some semi-professional, clerical.
- *Credit history:* Excellent, or mending after an unfortunate bout with spending.
- *Primary mode of transportation:* Automobile, probably newer.
- *Present living arrangement:* Possibly still at home, or in substandard apartment because of budget constraints.
- *Location of present home:* Probably close to the neighborhood, perhaps just across the line in the city.
- *Reason for moving:* Looking for better apartment that will reflect higher earning potential.
- *Expectations for a new apartment:* Modern, clean, affordable.

The second type of prospective tenant is older, single or married, with a good credit history and a long rental history. On a fixed income—pension, disability, or Social Security—their earnings limit the amount that can be spent on rent. But, like their younger counterparts, they wish to live in a stable neighborhood and are unable to afford the most desirable apartments.

The Profile:

- *Marital status:* Single or married.
- *Age:* 50-70.

- *Income:* Low, fixed income.
- *Type of employment:* No longer working.
- *Credit history:* Excellent.
- *Primary mode of transportation:* Public transportation.
- *Present living arrangement:* Substandard apartment because of budget constraints, or better quality apartment but must leave because of rent increases.
- *Location of present home:* Probably close to the neighborhood, perhaps just across the line in the city.
- *Reason for moving:* Present apartment is substandard, looking for something better; present apartment is too expensive, looking for something just as good but less expensive.
- *Expectations for a new apartment:* Modern, clean, affordable.

### How to Market Apartments in Building A

To appeal to these prospective tenants, the apartments in Building A must be in perfect condition, with spotlessly clean kitchens and baths, freshly shampooed carpets and freshly painted walls. Rents must be below market for the area, reflecting good value for the money. The building must be kept clean and in good repair, with a few extra niceties like brass numbers and knockers on the doors. The building should impart a feeling of class without being too glitzy. Make the best of every advantage the building offers.

## Faded Luxury in a Changing Neighborhood

Building B is a three-story walk-up more than 80 years old, a 24-unit building in a declining neighborhood that was originally an upper middle class area. Most of the surrounding homes are more than 60 years old, large, and obviously custom built. The neighborhood includes many mature trees and nice lawns. Houses are generally set back off the street, although the lots tend to be rather narrow.

The area includes a large number of apartment buildings, most of which are three-story walk-ups of 12 to 40 units. Apartments tend to be large and spacious, with many of the amenities one would expect in a building designed originally for an upper middle class population. The area tends to be highly congested, with parking difficult to find. Competition for tenants among the apartment buildings is fierce, with many buildings advertising vacancies year-round.

In the 1960s, the area attracted a large number of younger, single people. Although stable for many years, the neighborhood is now undergoing a period of decline. Some gangs are moving in and the traffic in drugs is increasing. Break-ins and other criminal activity is on the rise. While not yet considered to be an unsafe neighborhood, safety and security are certainly a consideration.

**Profile of the Neighborhood:**

- *Housing stock:* Mixed single-family and larger multi-family. Mostly walk-ups, but a few elevator buildings. Some of the older buildings have been rehabbed.

- *Density:* High density.

- *Age group:* Mixed, with older residents living in the many beautiful homes and younger residents living in the apartment buildings.

- *Family Status:* Most children in the area are from lower socio-economic groups. Higher economic residents tend to be older, with grown children who have left the area, or younger single individuals.

- *Socio-economic factors:* A growing number of residents are from the lowest socio-economic groups. Low rents in the area, which for many years attracted students and young professionals, now attract poorer tenants.

- *Reputation:* The area is changing, and the number of problems is growing. Still, it is a good area to obtain nice housing for low rents.

- *Safety:* Security is a major consideration in most of the area.

**Profile of Building B:**

- *Location:* The building is located on a lovely tree-lined residential street, only one block from Lake Michigan.

- *Characteristics of the building:* Three-story walk-up, with four separate entrances. The building is brick with many signs of age. Owners through the years have been reluctant to maintain the building in its original condition. Consequently, former balconies have been removed and other architectural niceties have been covered over or allowed to deteriorate. There is no front yard; grass in the back yard is mowed, but otherwise the yard is not well kept. Some tenants have tried to grow flowers, but with little success. The first floor units are commercial: a laundromat, a beauty shop, a rental office, a shoe shop. Some store fronts have been leased for businesses that are not typically store-front operations. In those stores, the windows are covered over and the nature of the business is not obvious.

- *Advantages:*
  1. Apartments are spacious, with hardwood floors, french doors that let in much light, decorative fireplaces and other stylish amenities.
  2. Commuter train station is less than one block away, while bus service is only one block the other way.
  3. Large trees and lawns give the neighborhood a comfortable feel.
  4. There is a laundromat in the building.
  5. Rents are very low in comparison with similar size apartments throughout the city. Apartments are a good value.
  6. Small shops across the street provide essential shopping.

- *Disadvantages:*
  1. Apartments are older, with few attempts to modernize.
  2. The neighborhood is changing.

3. The first floor of the building is commercial. Because the area no longer supports small shops, many of the stores are inhabited by businesses that cover over the front windows.

**Profile of a Prospective Tenant:**

The area offers spacious apartments at reasonable rents, a better value than most other sections of the city. The best prospective tenant for this building is young—25 to 35—with a stable but low-paying job; "city-smart," willing to take some risks in order to obtain more space for a lower rent.

The Profile:

- *Marital status:* Single.

- *Age:* Young.

- *Income:* $12,000 to $20,000.

- *Type of employment:* Semi-professional, clerical, service.

- *Credit history:* Often non-existent. Otherwise mixed, with some late pays but no major problems.

- *Primary mode of transportation:* Public transportation.

- *Present living arrangement:* Living in substandard apartment or with roommate because of budget constraints. Alternatively, living in nicer apartment but searching for something as nice for lower rent.

- *Location of present home:* In the neighborhood, or in a similar but higher-priced neighborhood.

- *Reason for moving:* Looking for a better value. Looking for better security. Roommate is getting married.

- *Expectations for a new apartment:* Affordable, clean, safe.

### How to Market Apartments in Building B

Because rents are low, it is easy to attract undesirable low income tenants. A better quality tenant, however, is more difficult to attract. The building must be safe, with no undesirable tenants. The halls and common areas must be clean and well maintained. Apartments must be clean and in good repair. Rents should be kept at or below market. Emphasize transportation, neighborhood charm, security and amenities of the apartment.

# Market to the Best Possible Tenant

Top quality tenants exist in every neighborhood. The best tenants in one neighborhood, however, may bear little resemblance to the best tenants in another neighborhood. That is why, particularly when working with a building that is difficult to manage, it is critical to identify who the prospective customers are. Think of the best tenants as A tenants. They pay the rent on time, they cause no problems, they are quiet, they plan to live in the apartment a long time. A tenants help keep the building up; they attract other A tenants to the building.

The consequence of failing to attract A tenants is a building that enters a downward spiral: B tenants, who closely resemble A tenants, move into the building. They cause a few problems; they are a little noisier, they entertain a few friends who appear to be less desirable, they don't keep the apartment clean. These little problems cause A tenants to begin thinking of living elsewhere.

As the A tenants leave, they are replaced by other B tenants. Before long, even the B tenants, who were attracted to the nice building by A tenants, begin to look elsewhere. As they leave, they are replaced by C tenants, and the process continues.

Remember: A tenants attract other A tenants, while B tenants attract C tenants. Always identify and market to the A tenants.

# Chapter

# 3

# Establish a Price:
# What Can You Get for
# Your Apartments?

**M**arketing professionals know that the price of a product directly contributes to the success of a marketing campaign. The price one finally attaches to a particular item may have little to do with the actual cost of manufacturing the item, but has everything to do with the image the price produces. As an example, a marketing specialist once took control of a failed direct mail campaign to sell a self-help tax manual. He changed nothing but the price, which he doubled. The book sold out on the first mailing after the change. Prospective customers, assuming that the only good advice is expensive advice, would not purchase the book when it was priced too cheap.

Establishing the price of an apartment often involves such subtle determinations as well. Pricing the apartment too low might be just as damaging as pricing it too high. Therefore, simply looking in the paper to see what other landlords are charging for similar size apartments is not enough.

To determine how much rent to charge for an apartment, consider all of these factors:

- Rents that are being charged for similar apartments in the building

- Rents that are being charged for similar apartments in the neighborhood

- The current vacancy rate in the neighborhood

- Competition for tenants

- The condition of the apartment

- The size of the apartment

- The condition of the building

- Location

- Amenities

## Rents That Are Being Charged for Similar Apartments in the Building

As a rule of thumb, the rents in a building should be maintained at a consistent level. Tenants talk with each other, and they learn what other tenants are paying for similar apartments. A wide disparity can create feelings of resentment and can lead to problems. When comparing rents, consider factors that create differences in desirability, such as which floor the apartment is on (in a walk-up building, the higher floors are less desirable, while in an elevator building the opposite is often true), the view, the overall condition of the apartment, or whether the kitchen has been modernized. If the vacancy rate is relatively high, it sometimes helps to price one or two less desirable apartments at bargain rates in order to attract more inquiries.

## Rents That Are Being Charged for Similar Apartments in the Neighborhood

To establish the range of rents that are being charged for similar types of apartments in the neighborhood, look through the rental section of the local newspaper. If more than one newspaper serves the area, look through each of the papers.

If there are numerous apartments for rent, establish the high, the low, the average and the median rents for each size and type of apartment you are renting. Do this by making a list of the rents for each size of apartment, i.e., studio, one bedrooom, two bedroom, etc. (Example Figure 3–1) When all of the rents have been copied, locate the highest rent for each category, then the lowest. To calculate the average rent for a particular size apartment, add all of the rents in that category and divide the sum by the total number of apartments in the category (see Figure 3–2).

You now know the high, the low and the average rent for each type of apartment. One more figure can be helpful, though: the median rent, the one that falls in the middle—the rent that has an equal number of rents above it and below it. The median rent reveals where the rents cluster and whether a few very high or very low rents have distorted the average. To obtain the median rent, list all of the rents in order from high to low and find the figure that falls in the middle (Figure 3–3).

By knowing the high, the low, the average and the median rents in the area, you have all the information you need on competing rents.

## Current Vacancy Rate in the Area

Regardless of how much other landlords are asking for rent, if the vacancy rate in the area at the time you are offering your apartment is quite high, the competition for available tenants will also be high. You may need to offer a lower rent, a rebate, a reduction in security deposit, or some other incentive to attract tenants to your building.

## Figure 3-1: High and Low Rents in the Area

### LIST OF RENTALS AVAILABLE IN THE AREA
(Taken from one issue of the weekly community newspaper)

### STUDIO

| | | | | | | | | | | |
|---|---|---|---|---|---|---|---|---|---|---|
| 395 | 415 | 390 | 435 | 395 | 420 | 425 | 400 | 480 | 465 | 365 |
| 360 | 395 | 400 | 425 | 350 | 390 | 390 | 440 | 250 | | |

High rent = $480     Low rent = $250

### 1 BEDROOM

| | | | | | | | | | | |
|---|---|---|---|---|---|---|---|---|---|---|
| 465 | 625 | 515 | 495 | 499 | 495 | 550 | 560 | 490 | 550 | 485 |
| 575 | 750 | 450 | 600 | 525 | 625 | 485 | 475 | 450 | 535 | 555 |
| 430 | 470 | 450 | 465 | 475 | 575 | 460 | 490 | 520 | 495 | 485 |
| 675 | 620 | 475 | 525 | 485 | 500 | 650 | 550 | 485 | 535 | 560 |
| 575 | 415 | 475 | 780 | 475 | 600 | 550 | 675 | 350 | 525 | 425 |
| 450 | 510 | 540 | 710 | 565 | 525 | 635 | 655 | 475 | 585 | 485 |
| 485 | 520 | 625 | 470 | 530 | 495 | 555 | 465 | 595 | 550 | 480 |
| 495 | 530 | 595 | 435 | 565 | 540 | 475 | 545 | 450 | 490 | 525 |
| 575 | 635 | 495 | 580 | 490 | | | | | | |

High rent = $780     Low rent = $350

### 2 BEDROOM

| | | | | | | | | | | |
|---|---|---|---|---|---|---|---|---|---|---|
| 695 | 700 | 645 | 560 | 725 | 725 | 600 | 750 | 685 | 850 | 665 |
| 725 | 555 | 595 | 800 | 725 | 790 | 1200 | 685 | 850 | 650 | 800 |
| 820 | 600 | 655 | 635 | 625 | 675 | 775 | 500 | 785 | 620 | 650 |
| 850 | 735 | 720 | 750 | 815 | 760 | 660 | 650 | 550 | 665 | 700 |
| 675 | 625 | 730 | 715 | 795 | 750 | 645 | 550 | | | |

High rent = $1200     Low rent = $500

### 3 BEDROOM

| | | | | | | | | | | |
|---|---|---|---|---|---|---|---|---|---|---|
| 850 | 675 | 650 | 1050 | 1200 | 1175 | 600 | 885 | 960 | 760 | 1100 |
| 1210 | 700 | 890 | | | | | | | | |

High rent = $1210     Low rent = $600

## Figure 3–2: Average Rents in the Area

### STUDIO

| | | | | | | | | | | |
|---|---|---|---|---|---|---|---|---|---|---|
| 395 | 415 | 390 | 435 | 395 | 420 | 425 | 400 | 480 | 465 | 365 |
| 360 | 395 | 400 | 425 | 350 | 390 | 390 | 440 | 250 | | |

Average Studio rent:

7,985 ÷ 20 = $399

### 1 BEDROOM

| | | | | | | | | | | |
|---|---|---|---|---|---|---|---|---|---|---|
| 465 | 625 | 515 | 495 | 499 | 495 | 550 | 560 | 490 | 550 | 485 |
| 575 | 750 | 450 | 600 | 525 | 625 | 485 | 475 | 450 | 535 | 555 |
| 430 | 470 | 450 | 465 | 475 | 575 | 460 | 490 | 520 | 495 | 485 |
| 675 | 620 | 475 | 525 | 485 | 500 | 650 | 550 | 485 | 535 | 560 |
| 575 | 415 | 475 | 780 | 475 | 600 | 550 | 675 | 350 | 525 | 425 |
| 450 | 510 | 540 | 710 | 565 | 525 | 635 | 655 | 475 | 585 | 485 |
| 485 | 520 | 625 | 470 | 530 | 495 | 555 | 465 | 595 | 550 | 480 |
| 495 | 530 | 595 | 435 | 565 | 540 | 475 | 545 | 450 | 490 | 525 |
| 575 | 635 | 495 | 580 | 490 | | | | | | |

Average 1 Bedroom rent:

49,409 ÷ 93 = $531

### 2 BEDROOM

| | | | | | | | | | | |
|---|---|---|---|---|---|---|---|---|---|---|
| 695 | 700 | 645 | 560 | 725 | 725 | 600 | 750 | 685 | 850 | 665 |
| 725 | 555 | 595 | 800 | 725 | 790 | 1200 | 685 | 850 | 650 | 800 |
| 820 | 600 | 655 | 635 | 625 | 675 | 775 | 500 | 785 | 620 | 650 |
| 850 | 735 | 720 | 750 | 815 | 760 | 660 | 650 | 550 | 665 | 700 |
| 675 | 625 | 730 | 715 | 795 | 750 | 645 | 550 | | | |

Average 2 Bedroom rent:

36,655 ÷ 52 = $705

### 3 BEDROOM

| | | | | | | | | | | |
|---|---|---|---|---|---|---|---|---|---|---|
| 850 | 675 | 650 | 1050 | 1200 | 1175 | 600 | 885 | 960 | 760 | 1100 |
| 1210 | 700 | 890 | | | | | | | | |

Average 3 Bedroom rent:

12,705 ÷ 14 = $908

## Figure 3–3: Analysis of Area Rents

### STUDIO

| | | | | | | | | | | |
|---|---|---|---|---|---|---|---|---|---|---|
| 250 | 350 | 360 | 365 | 390 | 390 | 390 | 395 | 395 | 395 | 400 |
| 400 | 415 | 420 | 425 | 425 | 435 | 440 | 465 | 480 | | |

Total number of rents in this category = 20

High rent = $480   Average rent = $399   Median rent = $395   Low rent = $250

### 1 BEDROOM

| | | | | | | | | | | |
|---|---|---|---|---|---|---|---|---|---|---|
| 350 | 415 | 425 | 430 | 435 | 450 | 450 | 450 | 450 | 450 | 460 |
| 465 | 465 | 465 | 470 | 470 | 475 | 475 | 475 | 475 | 475 | 475 |
| 475 | 480 | 485 | 485 | 485 | 485 | 485 | 485 | 485 | 490 | 490 |
| 490 | 490 | 495 | 495 | 495 | 495 | 495 | 495 | 499 | 500 | 510 |
| 515 | 520 | 520 | 525 | 525 | 525 | 525 | 525 | 530 | 530 | 535 |
| 535 | 540 | 540 | 545 | 550 | 550 | 550 | 550 | 550 | 555 | 555 |
| 560 | 560 | 565 | 565 | 575 | 575 | 575 | 575 | 580 | 585 | 595 |
| 595 | 600 | 600 | 620 | 625 | 625 | 625 | 635 | 635 | 650 | 655 |
| 675 | 675 | 710 | 750 | 780 | | | | | | |

Total number of rents in this category = 93

High rent = $780   Average rent = $531   Median rent = $520   Low rent = $350

### 2 BEDROOM

| | | | | | | | | | | |
|---|---|---|---|---|---|---|---|---|---|---|
| 500 | 550 | 550 | 555 | 560 | 595 | 600 | 600 | 620 | 625 | 625 |
| 635 | 645 | 645 | 650 | 650 | 650 | 655 | 660 | 665 | 665 | 675 |
| 675 | 685 | 685 | 695 | 700 | 700 | 715 | 720 | 725 | 725 | 725 |
| 725 | 730 | 735 | 750 | 750 | 750 | 760 | 775 | 785 | 790 | 795 |
| 800 | 800 | 815 | 820 | 850 | 850 | 850 | 1200 | | | |

Total number of rents in this category = 52

High rent = $1200   Average rent = $705   Median rent = $695   Low rent = $500

### 3 BEDROOM

| | | | | | | | | | | |
|---|---|---|---|---|---|---|---|---|---|---|
| 600 | 650 | 675 | 700 | 760 | 850 | 885 | 890 | 960 | 1050 | 1100 |
| 1175 | 1200 | 1210 | | | | | | | | |

Total number of rents in this category = 14

High rent = $1210   Average rent = $908   Median rent = $885   Low rent = $600

## The Condition of the Apartment

It is always best to make the apartment as attractive as possible. A fresh coat of paint, floors that are in good condition, appliances that are clean and in good working order, and new shades or mini-blinds will make an apartment extremely marketable (Chapter 5). If, in spite of all that, the apartment—because of age and prior inattention—does not show as well as the competition, the rent level will have to be adjusted. If, on the other hand, the apartment can be made to look spectacular, a higher rent can be charged.

## The Size of the Apartment

If the apartment is spacious, with lots of floor space and closets, a higher rent can be charged. Likewise, a small cramped apartment must be rented at a lower rate.

## The Condition of the Building

No matter how the apartment looks, if the building looks forbidding the rents will have to be adjusted. If the building looks spectacular, however, the condition of the apartment may not be as important.

## Location

Location often establishes the level of rent that can be charged for an apartment. A highly desirable location will translate into higher rents. Likewise, a location that is less desirable attracts lower rents. Consider such factors as proximity to schools, shopping, major transportation routes, on-street parking and parks. Also consider the desirability of the neighborhood.

## Amenities

In addition to all of the above, consider the specific amenities this apartment has to offer. Does it have a balcony, large closets, a modern kitchen, a modern bath? Is the bath ceramic tile? Is there parking? Is it a sunny apartment? Does it offer beautiful hardwood floors or plush carpet? Is there more than one bathroom? Are there laundry facilities? These are all questions that must be taken into account when comparing your apartment with other apartments on the market.

## Know the Competition

Renting apartments is like any other retail business. A product is offered to a potential buyer in a competitive market. To be successful, you must know the competition. After looking through the newspaper and establishing comparable rent levels, go look at a few apartments as if you were a prospective tenant. Drive by a few others to learn about such factors as location, the condition of the building, etc. After driving through the neighborhood and seeing a few apartments, you will know how your product compares with that of the competition.

## Test the Market

If you have a little time before the apartment has to be rented, try testing the market by offering the apartment at a higher rent than the competition. If, on the other hand, time is short—and in the rental business, time is money—offer the apartment at a lower rent than the competition to attract tenants quickly.

## Supply and Demand

The factor to keep in mind when establishing a rent is the law of supply and demand. If demand is high and supply is low, a commodity can be sold at a high price. If, however, supply is high and demand is low, prices will be much lower. When establishing a rent, therefore, determine the demand for the product, know the competition, and establish a rent that reflects those factors.

# Chapter
# 4

# Attract the Best Tenants with Effective Advertising

Finding the ideal tenant requires advertising. The best product in the world will remain unsold if no one knows about it. Advertising should be cost effective: the money spent should attract the largest possible response for the least possible cost. Cost-effective does not always mean the lowest priced ad or the cheapest newspaper, however. Sometimes an expensive newspaper ad is the most cost-effective advertising. Other times a simple sign in the window does the job. A building can be its own best advertisement, requiring little more than a small notice of vacancy to attract a stream of prospective tenants. Other buildings require other forms of advertising, the most common being newspaper ads and for rent signs.

## Referrals

The best advertisement for a good product is often word of mouth. People talk to their friends and relatives about items they purchase, about their cars, about the workers they employ and most of all about their homes. And people talk particularly about their landlords.

Unfortunately, when the landlord becomes the topic of conversation, the talk all too often centers around unresponsiveness and inconsiderateness. A landlord who offers a top-quality apartment, excellent service, and a safe, clean, quiet building is more likely to be the exception than the rule. People like to talk about exceptional things, however, and they particularly like to brag if their living situation is better than a friend's. In many cases, they also like to encourage their friends to share their good fortune by moving into the same building.

This kind of informal referral system should be encouraged by rewarding tenants who refer top-quality prospects. If a tenant refers a friend to the building, send a note thanking them for introducing such a top-quality tenant (Figure 4–1). Along with the note send the tenant a certificate worth $50 toward a future rent payment (Figure 4–2). If $50 seems overly generous, keep in mind that the cost of running one ad in a metropolitan newspaper for one week often exceeds that amount.

## Newspaper Ads

While word of mouth advertising can be effective and cost-efficient, it normally is not enough to keep a building full. Additional advertising usually is necessary. The two most common forms of advertising are newspaper ads and signs at the building. By far the most effective of the two is a well-written newspaper ad.

### Writing an Effective Newspaper Ad

The majority of newspaper ads list only the size of the apartment, the date when available, the rent, and a phone number (Figure 4.3). In a newspaper with a small rental section, such an ad may be effective. If demand for apartments is high, moreover, that kind of minimal advertising can attract an adequate selection of prospective tenants.

## Figure 4–1: Thank You Note for a Referral

September 10, 1992

Herbert Fall
4567 Spring Court, Apt. 5C
Chicago IL 60000

Dear Mr. Fall:

Just a note to say thanks for encouraging your friend, Delores Seasons, to become a tenant in our building.

When tenants feel confident enough to encourage their friends to live in the building it indicates they take real pride in the building. And such referrals allow us to maintain the best possible community of tenants.

As a gesture of our appreciation, please accept the enclosed certificate worth $50.00 discount on one rent payment. Use it any time you choose by enclosing it with your reduced rent payment for the month.

Very truly yours,

John Winters

## Figure 4–2

---

**$50**   *REDUCED RENT CERTIFICATE*   **$50**

*This certificate is worth $50.00 toward the payment of one month's rent.
Spend it any time you wish. Simply subtract $50.00 from your rent
and enclose this certificate with your payment.*

Name_____Apartment _____

Validated by_____

**$50**   *SPRING COURT APARTMENTS*   **$50**

---

## Figure 4–3: Basic Newspaper Ad

**5550 N. KENMORE
Studio $325, all util incld
312-275-9000**

---

Most often, however, competition for good tenants is high and an ad, to be effective, must be written very carefully. The best ads should accomplish these three results:

- Attract the reader's attention

- Hold the reader's interest

- Pique the reader's excitement

## *How to Attract the Reader's Attention*

Look at a page from the classified section of your local newspaper. Typically you see a dense mass of copy, organized into columns. In the middle of that sea of words, how will a reader find your ad? When an ad is lost among hundreds of other non-descript words and phrases, the reader must carefully read through many ads to uncover yours. If the reader's eye is drawn immediately to your ad, however, it will likely be read before the others in the column. To grab the reader's attention, several tricks can be used.

### White Space

As you look at the classified page, where is your eye drawn? To the spots where the dense type has been broken by patches of white. Many of the commercial ads allow for a great deal of white space. These ads are typically designed by a professional and submitted in "camera-ready" form. Such a process is expensive and, for your purposes, unnecessary. You can accomplish much the same thing by designing the ad copy to allow for white space.

One technique is to leave the first and last lines blank. Tell the ad taker that the first line is to be blank. Begin the copy on the second line, then leave the final line blank. Presto! White space.

Another trick is to ask the ad taker to place an "x" at the beginning and the end of the first line, and at the beginning and end of the last line. The four x's create a box effect and leave white space in the ad.

A third trick: Make the first and last lines into a row of stars, or boxes, or asterisks, or x's, depending on what characters the ad taker has available. This separates your ad from the dense copy surrounding it.

### Visual Grabbers

After leaving white space to draw the reader's eye, the first line of type should grab the reader's attention. Use larger letters if possible, center the words, and use bold type. If the first line of the ad is blank, place a line of stars on either side of the lead words in the second line.

## Location

Some classified sections alphabetize ads by the first word in the ad, giving you some control over the location of your ad. For the ad to appear as close to the beginning of the section as possible, write the ad so that the first word begins with the letter "a," preferably followed by another "a" or a "b." An example: AAA Building!

## *Hold the Reader's Interest*

Once your ad has gained the readers' attention, it must hold the readers' interest. Do this with the first few words of the ad copy. Some likely first lines would be: "Special rates," "Off-Season Special," "A Gorgeous Building," "Safe, Clean Building."

## *Pique the Reader's Excitement*

After gaining the readers' interest, make them excited about your apartment by emphasizing its features. The features you list, of course, will depend upon who your targeted customer is.

Make a list of all the advantages this apartment has to offer, for example:

- Public transportation
- Hardwood floors
- French doors
- Wonderful view
- Desirable location
- Fully carpeted
- Utilities included
- Patio
- Balconies
- Large cabinet kitchen
- Ceramic tile bath

The list, of course, could go on.

Decide which of these attractions is most likely to appeal to your targeted customer and feature them in the ad. Limit the number to three or four.

## Include the Price

An effective ad should appeal primarily to the targeted customer. One of the criteria that defines your targeted customer is price. If the price is in the ad, it selects out those prospects who cannot afford the rent or do not wish to spend that amount.

## What about the Address?

Some property managers recommend including the address so that prospective tenants can drive past the property before calling. Others feel that requiring the prospective tenant to call for the address provides an opportunity to begin the selling process. As a rule of thumb, if either the physical features or the specific location of the building is a primary attraction, include the address. Otherwise, list a phone number and approximate location.

## Use a Phone Number That Will Be Answered

When prospective tenants call about an apartment, they need to reach a person who knows about the apartment and can set up an appointment to see it. Do not rely on an answering machine to take messages. The majority of the persons calling will be looking at several apartments. If they fail to reach you, your apartment will not be among the ones they visit on that day. By the time you are able to return the call, a decision may already have been made. Include a second phone number if necessary to assure that a live voice answers the phone.

## The Cost of Newspaper Ads

Newspaper ads can be quite costly. As in any business, however, the cost of advertising is justified by the amount of business that is generated through the advertising. Do not scrimp on the size or frequency of a newspaper ad in order to save money. Spend what is necessary to attract the best kind of tenant. The pay-off will come when the phone is ringing off the hook and prospective tenants are competing with one another for the privilege of living in your building.

# Signs

### The Front Door Sign

Many of the best prospective tenants first select a neighborhood in which they wish to live and then search for an apartment in that neighborhood. Rather than look through the paper, they often drive through a neighborhood to see what apartments are available. A well-crafted sign on the building can be effective in attracting this kind of tenant. Two types of signs are commonly used. One is a small sign that is taped to the front door, a sign that notifies persons walking or driving past that apartments are available in the building. The size of the sign requires that the prospect walk up to the front door to obtain the details. (See example, Figure 4–4) If the apartment is located in an attractive, highly desirable building, this kind of sign can be particularly effective. Prospects already know that they like the building and the location. All that is left is to sell them the apartment itself. In a tough rental market, however, such a sign may not compete for attention with some of the larger signs in the neighborhood.

### The "For Rent" Sign

A larger sign, one that is attached to the building or placed in the yard, will often attract more attention than the small door sign, particularly from persons who are driving past and are drawn by the sign to look at the building. Some persons may not have considered changing apartments before noticing your sign.

If a large sign is used, it should be professionally made: no hand lettered signs; no plastic "for rent" signs. The sign must be large enough to be read easily from the road. Like the newspaper ad, the sign must do three things: attract attention, hold the reader's attention, and whet the reader's appetite.

To attract attention, the sign should be colorful and well designed; tasteful, not garish; and located so that it can be seen easily.

## Figure 4–4

# FOR RENT
# IN THIS BUILDING

| SIZE | FLOOR | AVAILABLE | RENT |
|------|-------|-----------|------|
| 1 BEDROOM | 3RD | SEPTEMBER 1 | $575 |
| 2 BEDROOM | 4TH | OCTOBER 1 | $755 |
| STUDIO | 1ST | IMMEDIATELY | $490 |

CONTACT JOHN WINTERS

555-4488

OR

RING APARTMENT 3C for BUILDING MANAGER

To hold the reader's attention, the first line must be in large print and convey an idea that will encourage the reader to read the rest of the sign. Use phrases such as: "Beautiful Modern Apartment," "Sparkling Clean Apartment," "Old World Charm," etc. The sign need not say "Apartment for Rent." This would be redundant.

To encourage the reader to call, the sign should include one or two of the prime attractions the building offers. Be careful, however, not to fill the sign too full. A sign with too much information cannot be read by someone driving past. The goal is to encourage a prospective tenant to call for more information, not to convey everything about the apartment on the sign.

### *Permanent Signs*

Some property managers like to post a permanent sign at the building, indicating the types of apartments that are available and a phone number to be called. When the building is full, a small sign is often added, motel-like, that indicates "No Vacancy." Such signs are so generic as to be practically useless: it is never clear whether an apartment is available; a potential  tenant must call to inquire about vacancies. In a competitive market, most prospects will simply pass. The other problem with permanent signs is that tenants in the building may get the idea there  are permanent vacancies in the building, and they may wonder why.

If a permanent sign is used, it should give only the name of the building, the address, and the name and phone number of the property manager. It should be small and tasteful, and designed to fit with the appearance of the building.

## Apartment Rental Agencies

Rental agencies can be found in most cities. Their primary business is matching tenants with apartments. Typically the fee for locating a tenant is a percentage—normally 50 percent to 100 percent—of the first month's rent. At first glance, the idea seems like a good one: the agency advertises, takes the application, completes the background check, shows the apartment and delivers a qualified tenant, relieving the landlord from any such obligations. The agency collects either the first month's rent, or the first month's rent plus a security deposit, from which they subtract their fee.

A word of caution, however: the rental agency's goal is different from your goal. Their goal is to rent an apartment and collect a commission. Your goal is to rent the apartment to the *best possible tenant*. The difference is significant.

The rental agency is not as motivated as you are to do a thorough and complete background check on the applicant. Why should they be? They will suffer none of the consequences of making a poor decision, and every prospective tenant who is disqualified is one less commission for the agency. Keep in mind that the relationship between the rental agency and the prospective tenant ends when the lease is signed and the fee is collected, while your relationship with the new tenant has just begun. You want a tenant who will pay the rent on time every month, a tenant who will stay in the apartment for a while, a tenant who will not cause problems in the building or damage to the apartment. You are the best person to judge whether a prospective tenant will fill those criteria.

A second word of caution: a rental agency handles many buildings and, therefore, may steer a tenant away from your building toward another building that may be easier to rent. Additionally, some rental agencies have been known to be less than honest in their dealings with prospective tenants. (Some dishonestly declare that they have hundreds of listings when, in fact, most of their listings are simply ads they pull from the newspaper which the prospective tenant could easily do without paying a huge fee. Although this may not effect you directly, these kinds of agencies can cloud the industry as a whole, thereby driving away some of the best potential tenants.

If you choose to work with a rental agency, take some precautions. Insist on retaining the right to complete your own background and credit check on any prospective tenant, as well as the right to interview the applicant personally. Then insist on the right to refuse any applicant brought to you by the agency. Even with such safeguards in place, continue to use caution in all your dealings with the agency. They might in fact become your ally, but they could also cause untold problems.

# Chapter

# 5

# Prepare the Apartment to Attract the Best Tenants

The goal of effective property management is to attract and keep the best possible tenants. Good tenants have their choice of places to live; they choose only the best within their price range. If an apartment is dirty or otherwise in poor condition, the best tenants will go elsewhere. Even in a market when apartments are easy to rent, the best tenants always gravitate toward the best apartments.

Why look for the best tenants? Once they find a suitable apartment, good tenants tend to stay put. This longevity translates into significant savings for the owner: lower redecorating costs, lower advertising costs, and a lower vacancy rate. For those reasons, the apartment you show must be among the best in order to compete for the best tenants.

## Only Show a Perfect Apartment

Perfect means that the apartment is in the best possible condition it can be in. It does not mean the apartment has been remodeled or reconditioned. When a prospective tenant first walks into the apartment, it should immediately look bright, spacious and clean. You should feel proud of the apartment when you show it, secure in the knowledge that this apartment is probably the cleanest and the best kept that this particular prospect has seen or will see.

This first impression is the most important. Most tenants cannot visualize what an apartment might look like when it is cleaned or repaired, even though you promise them it will be. All they see are the smudges on the walls, the cracks in the ceilings, or the broken tile in the bathroom and they want to leave. Most prospective tenants are also doubting Thomases, having experienced broken promises from landlords in the past. They rightfully wonder whether the promises you make will be kept.

## Before Showing It, Make Sure the Apartment Is in Good Repair

To prepare an apartment for showing, first make a list of the repairs that must be made. Use the Apartment Preparation List (Figure 5–1) as a guide. Then hire competent workers who will complete the work quickly and do the job right.

- *Walls:* Walls should look freshly painted and free of cracks or holes. Use the same paint in all apartments: off-white flat for the living room, bedroom and dining room walls, semi-gloss for the trim—either the same color as the walls or, if you prefer, white for the trim. Put semi-gloss on the kitchen and bathroom walls. When apartments are painted with the same paint, the walls can often be touched up rather than completely re-painted, which saves a lot of money. Use a good quality paint but not necessarily the best or the most expensive. A

## Figure 5–1

## APARTMENT PREPARATION CHECKLIST

Building _____

Apt. _____ Occupancy Date _____

1st Inspection Date _____

2nd Inspection Date _____

In each room, indicate which items need to be
repaired (R), replaced (X), painted (P), or cleaned (C)

### LIVING ROOM

Walls and Ceiling _____

Floor _____

Baseboard and Trim _____

Doors _____

Windows _____

Closet _____

Electrical _____

Misc _____

### DINING ROOM

Walls and Ceiling _____

Floor _____

Baseboard and Trim _____

Doors _____

Windows _____

Closet _____

Electrical _____

Misc _____

### _____ BEDROOM

Walls and Ceiling _____

Floor _____

Baseboard and Trim _____

Doors _____

Windows _____

Closet _____

Electrical _____

Misc _____

### _____ BEDROOM

Walls and Ceiling _____

Floor _____

Baseboard and Trim _____

Doors _____

Windows _____

Closet _____

Electrical _____

Misc _____

### BATHROOM

Walls and Ceiling _____

Floor _____

Baseboard and Trim _____

Door _____

Window _____

Closet _____

Electrical _____

Plumbing _____

Fixtures _____

Misc _____

### KITCHEN

Walls and Ceiling _____

Floor _____

Baseboard and Trim _____

Doors _____

Windows _____

Closet _____

Cabinets _____

Plumbing _____

Appliances _____

Electrical _____

SPECIAL INSTRUCTIONS: _____

_____

_____

contractor's grade is ideal. Buy the paint in five-gallon pails to obtain the best price.

- *Floors:* Floors must be in excellent repair, with no broken tile, no worn or stained carpet, and no darkened and scarred hardwood floors. Hire a professional to sand and refinish hardwood floors if they need it. Shop around for a good price; the cost is usually less than the price of new carpet. If there are worn areas, it is often possible to touch them up and revarnish the entire floor without sanding. Install new carpeting if the present carpet is worn or badly stained. If it is in good condition, have the carpet shampooed by a professional using water extraction equipment. Replace any broken or loose floor tiles. If necessary, recover tiled floors with no-wax tile or linoleum.

- *Appliances:* Appliances must be in good working condition, without missing or loose handles, knobs or trays. Replace caked or rusted burner pans with new ones. Replace broken or missing knobs. If any of the appliances is badly scratched or dented, replace it. Shop around for a good used appliance dealer who will install reconditioned appliances for a fraction of the cost of new.

- *Plumbing:* Repair dripping faucets or running toilets. Be sure the toilet flushes, the faucets have adequate water pressure, and the drains flow freely.

- *Ceramic tile:* Repair broken ceramic tile; regrout tile if necessary to remove dark spots in the grout. Such spots typically indicate moisture is seeping through. Failure to correct the problem not only leaves unsightly spots in the bathroom or kitchen, but leads to more expensive repairs later.

- *Electrical:* Replace broken or missing parts from light fixtures. Inexpensive replacement parts are usually available from hardware stores or do-it-yourself lumber yards. If a light fixture cannot be repaired, replace it. Replace broken switches and electrical outlets.

- *Windows:* Repair broken, cracked or discolored window glass. Repair torn or broken screens. Check the storm windows and screens to be sure they all work easily. If not, make them work. Replace broken, torn or stained shades or blinds. Install new ones if none are there.

## Never Show a Dirty Apartment

After all the repairs have been completed, hire a professional to clean the apartment thoroughly, including the bathroom, kitchen, appliances, light fixtures, floors and any other part of the apartment that needs cleaning. Be certain there are no strange smells, that the apartment looks and smells sparkling clean when a prospective tenant walks in.

## Turn On the Utilities

Before showing an apartment, be certain that the electricity is turned on and that all the electrical fixtures and appliances are in good working order. Check that there is a working light in every room. If a room has no ceiling fixture, install a lamp that can be turned on. Do not show a darkened room.

## What If You Have Several Vacant Apartments and Limited Funds?

If you have several apartments to be rented and limited funds for readying them, pick one to use as a model. The model apartment should be absolutely perfect. Show the model first, so that the prospect knows how thorough you will be in preparing the other apartments. Then, after the prospect is convinced, show one or two vacant apartments—no more. Although these apartments might not be painted and some repairs remain to be completed, they should nevertheless be clean. Never show a dirty apartment!

If the tenant likes one of the vacant apartments, offer to include in the lease a list of all improvements that will be made. Ask the tenant to point out any items they would like to see added to the list. If a request is reasonable include it, even if it is something you would not routinely do. If the tenant requests an item that is more expensive than you like, offer to share the cost. Participating in decisions about the apartment imparts a feeling of pride and ownership to the tenant.

## Know Your Prospective Tenant and Decorate Accordingly

To attract the best tenants, decorate apartments in a manner that will be most attractive to them. Learn the preferences of your targeted customer. In some neighborhoods tenants place a premium on carpeted floors, while in others tenants search for hardwood floors. Among some prospective tenants, mini-blinds are *de rigueur* and ceiling fans are essential, while others prefer the more traditional window shade and drapery rod and have no use for ceiling fans.

Before preparing an apartment, learn about the neighborhood and the expectations of the residents who live there. Then do everything possible to meet those expectations. If hardwood floors are the rule in the neighborhood, show them hardwood floors if you have them. If carpet is a mark of luxury, carpet the floors. If mini-blinds are the rage, give them mini-blinds. Ceiling fans and mini-blinds are relatively inexpensive to install, particularly if they mean the difference between renting or not renting to an exceptional tenant.

Beware the old saw, "Penny-wise and pound foolish." Do not spend money recklessly in the pursuit of a good tenant, but do not refuse to spend money wisely to attract the best tenants. Having good tenants in the building pays off in many different ways. Spend a little at the beginning and enjoy the dividends of low turnover and reduced management problems for many years.

# Prepare the Building

One old-timer used to advise, "Walk the building every day." The advice is good. A landlord can become too accustomed to a building and overlook the details. Before prospective tenants see an apartment, they see the building. The best tenants will reject a building that appears to be undesirable. Walk the building, looking at it through the eyes of a prospective tenant. Look for the details that tenants look for, the details that reveal what kind of landlord they can expect:

- *Mailboxes:* In what condition are the mailboxes? Are they loose? Do some of the doors hang open? Are the names on the mailboxes in a consistent fashion? What kind of first impression do the mailboxes give to a prospective tenant: of a clean and well-kept building or a building that is neglected?

- *Hallways and stairs:* Are they clean, well painted, bright? Or is the carpet frayed and the curtains dirty? Is there dirt in the corners; and has the wax built up to a grimy, yellowed consistency?

- *Light fixtures:* Are they dirty? Are light bulbs burned out?

- *Windows:* Do they sparkle or are they encrusted with dirt?

Drive past the building and look at it from the street. Search for signs of neglect: peeling paint, trash in the yard, broken windows, torn screens. Stop in front of the building and look at it carefully. Does it invite a tenant inside, or does it seem foreboding?

If any part of the building conveys a sense of neglect or danger, correct the problem. The only way a prospective tenant may see an apartment is by passing through the front door of the building. If the best tenants turn away without passing through the front door, the only prospects left are substandard tenants, and the building will suffer from high turnover, high vacancy rates, high costs for maintenance and repair, and a continuing decline in the quality of the tenant population.

# Chapter

# 6

# The Selling Begins When the Telephone Rings

**E**ffective marketing causes the telephone to ring. Attracted by the advertising, prospective tenants call to inquire about the vacant apartment, which is ready to dazzle anyone who walks through the door. But the apartment, as nice as it is, will not sell itself. That job remains to be done and you are the salesperson. Selling the apartment begins when a prospective tenant places the first call. The conversation, innocent as it seems, is really a short sales presentation, consisting of five distinct parts:

- Building excitement
- Qualifying the prospect
- Presenting the product
- Overcoming objections
- Closing the sale

## When the Phone Rings

The goal of this first phone call is to identify the callers who are good prospects and convince them to come see the apartment. But first, you must continue to build the excitement that led them to make the call. A prospective tenant calls about an apartment because his or her interest has been piqued. The first response to the caller should be designed to hold his or her interest and to make him or her even more excited about seeing the apartment.

When a prospect calls, the typical opening line is, "I'm calling about the apartment."

Rather than the typical response, "Okay. . . ." followed by a long pause, your response should be something like this: "Are you calling about the one-bedroom apartment with lots of closet space?" Or: "I'm happy you called. Are you looking for a sparkling clean apartment?"

If you are not comfortable with these lines, tailor some for yourself. Nevertheless, the goal is to build excitement from your first contact with a prospective tenant.

## Qualifying the Prospect

After the opening lines most callers will begin asking questions about the apartment.

"Where is it located?"

"How much is the rent?"

"Is it carpeted?"

Many, not knowing which questions to ask, will simply say, "Tell me about the apartment."

The best way to lose a sale is to allow a prospect to ask all the questions. The second best way to lose a sale, and to waste a lot of your own time in the bargain, is to begin pitching a product before determining the prospect's wants and needs. The goal of the first call is to determine whether this person is a good prospect and, if so, to convince them to view the apartment. Therefore, begin immediately to qualify the caller.

A prospective tenant who calls about an apartment wants to know whether this apartment will satisfy his or her needs. So do you.

Neither of you should waste time looking through an apartment that has no chance of fulfilling the prospective tenant's wishes or one that costs more than the prospect can afford.

Rather than simply answering the tenant's questions, therefore, ask some of your own. Attempt to gain control of the conversation with the questions you pose:

"What move-in date are you looking for?"

"How many persons will be living in the apartment?"

"Do you work in the area?"

"What size apartment are you looking for?"

"What things are important to you in an apartment?"

Follow each of the tenant's questions with a qualifying question of your own:

Tenant: "How much is the rent?"

Landlord: "The rent is $____. Does this fit your budget?"

Tenant: "What is the address?"

Landlord: "The address is _____. Are you familiar with that area?"

Tenant: "Is the apartment carpeted?"

Landlord: "Are you looking for a carpeted apartment?"

Tenant: "Is the heat included?"

Landlord: "Utilities are not included. Are you looking for a heated apartment?"

Tenant: "Is the apartment air-conditioned?"

Landlord: "Are you looking for an air-conditioned apartment?"

Make a list of the questions that will qualify a prospective tenant, then ask the questions when a prospect calls. If the questions determine that the tenant is not qualified, politely end the conversation. If, however, the prospect seems qualified for the apartment, proceed with the next step.

## Present the Product

If a caller seems qualified, the presentation should be a brief resume of the apartment's advantages, geared to the answers the prospect gave to the questions you posed. The presentation is then followed by a closing question.

"This is an ideal apartment for a young couple like you. The closets are huge and the living room is perfect for entertaining guests. Would you like to see it?"

"The location seems perfect for you: the commuter train is just down the street, and the shops in the neighborhood are within easy walking distance. When would you like to see the apartment?"

## Overcome Objections

When an otherwise qualified prospect objects to something about the apartment, attempt to overcome the objection by isolating it and determining how important the objection is:

*Objection:* "The rent is more than I want to spend."

*Response:* "If I were able to make the rent more attractive, would you be interested in the apartment?"

*Objection:* "The apartment sounds really beautiful, but I really want carpet in the living room and bedroom."

*Response:* "If we were able to carpet one or both of the rooms, would you be interested in the apartment?"

Isolating the objection reveals whether the objection is legitimate or just an excuse to get off the phone. Without committing to lowering the rent or carpeting the apartment, it is possible to convince the qualified tenant to view the apartment. After viewing your beautifully prepared apartment, the prospect might decide that area rugs will do just fine or that the apartment is worth a few dollars more a month.

## Close the Sale

During the first inquiry, the goal (the close) is to establish an appointment for a qualified prospect to view the apartment. At each step the path has been leading to the close. When the product was presented, a closing question was asked. If objections were raised and met, repeat the closing question:

"When would you like to see the apartment?"

"Is it better for you to see the apartment in the morning, or is an afternoon time better for you?"

"Would you like to schedule an appointment for you and your husband to see the apartment?"

If you have been successful, the outcome of the conversation will be an appointment to see the apartment.

# Chapter

# 7

# Don't Just Show the Apartment, Sell It!

When a prospective tenant arrives to view an apartment, everything possible has been done to make the apartment sell itself. The building sparkles; the apartment is gleaming. The prospective tenant has been preliminarily qualified: you know this apartment can fill his or her needs. Only one step remains in the marketing process: to sell the apartment.

Showing the apartment should include the same five steps that were followed during the inquiry call:

- Build excitement

- Qualify the prospect

- Present the product

- Overcome objections

- Close the sale

The goal now is to receive a completed application form and a deposit.

## Re-Qualify the Prospect

Begin immediately to engage the prospective tenant in conversation. While showing the apartment, review some of the questions that were covered in the inquiry call and ask others. Try to learn as much as possible about the prospect. Find out where the person is employed, how many people are in the family, how many people will be living in the apartment, what the move-in date would be. Ask what features are important in an apartment. Ask why the person is moving: perhaps this apartment offers something that was lacking in the previous apartment. Ask about pets.

After an effective qualification, the presentation will focus on those characteristics of the apartment that will most satisfy this particular prospect. Alternatively, if the apartment proves to be unsuitable after the qualification, offer a different apartment, if one exists, that comes closer to meeting the prospect's needs.

## The Presentation

When showing the apartment, accentuate the benefits this apartment has to offer. Don't simply point out the obvious, such as "This is the living room, this is the bathroom, etc." The presentation should be specifically focused on the needs and desires that were expressed during the qualification:

"In the summertime the cross-breeze created by the French doors can be very comfortable."

"The lay-out of this kitchen is particularly well-suited for a chef such as you."

"I just love the view out this window."

## Sell Yourself

It is not uncommon for a tenant to choose an apartment because they feel secure with the landlord. Most tenants have had experiences with inattentive landlords and are willing to give up some niceties and amenities in return for a landlord who will provide them with responsive services. To develop that kind of trust, show genuine interest in the prospective tenant. Ask questions about them, then gear the conversation to their interests. Additionally, point out specific ways in which you have been responsive to tenants' needs. Mention one or two satisfied tenants and what you did to satisfy them.

## Discover Specific Objections

Never allow a prospective tenant to walk out the door saying, "I'll be in touch," or "I'll call you later," or "I'll let you know."

Both during and after the presentation, ask the prospect for a response. If he or she is non-commital, try to elicit specific objections. A prospect who says "No thanks" without giving a reason allows no opportunity to neutralize his or her concerns. Many times a prospect's reasons for not renting are insignificant and easily challenged and overcome. If you do not know what they are, however, you have no chance to respond to them. Ask questions that will provoke a response:

"How does this compare with other apartments you have looked at?"

"How did you like the kitchen?"

"Is there anything in particular you didn't like?"

Often, you might uncover some minor something that stuck in the person's craw, something that can easily be rectified, something that would never have been expressed if you failed to ask.

On the other hand, the prospect might not like the apartment for reasons that cannot be overcome:

They may say, "Well, it's just too small," or "The bedroom's too small, my water bed would never fit," or "The bathroom is much too large, I'm looking for something more cozy," or "I need a southern exposure for my plants." In those cases, another apartment might fit the bill. If not, at least you know why they found the apartment undesirable, and this can help immeasurably in later marketing strategies.

## Overcome Objections

Entire sections of training manuals have been dedicated to the process of overcoming prospects' objections. Space does not permit a full discussion of all the techniques that can be used. There is one particular method, however, that can be effective when showing an apartment.

First, isolate the objection by asking this question: "Is that your only reason for not renting this apartment?"

If the answer is yes, respond to the objection. If other problems are expressed, make note of them and work on them one by one.

To neutralize an objection and to lead to a close, use an "If . . . then . . . " response:

"If I were to . . . (insert how the offending condition would be fixed or alleviated), then would you be interested in renting this apartment?"

If, for example, the prospect has complained that the bathroom has no shower, the response would be, "If we were to install a shower to your liking, would you take the apartment?"

If you were simply to say, "We can put in a shower," no response is called for, and the conversation can easily die. An "If . . . then . . ." question forces a commitment from the tenant that if a shower is installed, he or she will in fact rent the apartment.

Do not, of course, offer to make any changes that are unreasonable either because of expense or because the result would be a less attractive apartment. There are times, however, when a simple, low-cost alteration can result in renting an apartment to an excellent tenant

## Develop a Feeling of Urgency

A prospective tenant should not feel that they are the only ones interested in this apartment. During your conversation, let them know that "The phone has been ringing off the hook." Mention how many times you have shown the apartment. Tell them about your appointments later that day.

The object is to encourage them to make a decision and to leave a deposit.

### Closing the Sale

The critical part of every sales presentation is the close. As the pros say, "You must ask for the money."

To lead to the close, it is often effective to give the prospect a choice of two responses. If two apartments were shown, for example, ask, "Which of the two apartments did you like better?"

If the reply is, "Oh, I like apartment A better because of the view," your response is, "Why don't you fill out an application on apartment A and leave a deposit today? We can start the background and credit check immediately and let you know by Wednesday whether you qualify for the apartment."

Or this: "Would you like to leave an application and deposit today, or is it easier to drop it off tomorrow?"

An effective salesperson always knows how to ask for the close diplomatically: "Since you like the apartment so much, why not leave an application and deposit today to make sure you don't lose it?"

Never allow a prospect to leave saying, "I'll be in touch." Let them leave under one of two conditions: You know why they decided not to rent your apartment and there is no way you can overcome their objections, or they have left a completed application and a deposit to hold the apartment.

## Avoiding the No-Shows

One of the most time-consuming parts of renting an apartment is driving to the building, showing the apartment, then driving back home or to the office. The unfortunate truth is that as many as 60 percent of the prospective tenants who make appointments to see an apartment will not show up, no matter how well you qualified them on the phone.

One can speculate why this occurs: some callers discover what they want to know over the phone, make a decision that they are not interested, but are unable to say no when asked if they would like to see the apartment. Others learn the address, drive past, decide they do not like the building or the neighborhood and then do not keep the appointment. Still others are simply irresponsible and, after making an appointment, either change their minds or simply forget. Sometimes a prospect makes several appointments, finds an apartment to rent before seeing yours, but is not courteous enough to call and cancel.

The unfortunate fact is that prospects who show consideration for your time are extremely rare. Because of that, a majority of the people who make appointments to see an apartment will not keep the appointment. Fortunately, there are steps that can be taken to minimize the amount of wasted time waiting for non-showing prospects.

- *Tip #1:* Schedule specific times for showing the apartment and schedule all callers in one of those time slots. If you schedule more than one prospective tenant at one time, chances are that at least one will show up. Additionally, if more than one prospect does keep the appointment it creates a sense of urgency that can lead to a quicker decision.

- *Tip #2:* When a prospective tenant calls for an appointment, obtain the person's name, home phone number and work phone number. Prior to the appointment call the prospective tenant to confirm the appointment. This increases the chance that the prospect will show up for the appointment and eliminates waiting for the prospect who indicates they will not be there.

- *Tip #3:* Hire somebody on-sight to show apartments—someone you have trained in simple sales techniques. The best arrangement is for an on-sight manager or janitor to show apartments. If the janitor does not live in the building, offer a trusted tenant an incentive for showing apartments. In most cases, it is better to take all the phone calls yourself. (Remember, the selling begins when the first contact is made.) You can then qualify the prospects, giving the address and the janitor's phone number to those who qualify.

This plan only works under certain conditions, however. If the rental market is particularly difficult, or if you are working with a building that has trouble attracting good tenants, you may want to continue to show the apartments yourself so that you have some control over the quality of the salesmanship and the presentation.

# Section
# II
## New Tenants

**E**very time a landlord accepts a new tenant, the landlord takes a risk. The movie *Pacific Heights* offers a chilling example of the potential consequences of neglecting to check out a seemingly good tenant. In the movie, an earnest young couple, eager to find a tenant for one of the two extra apartments in their new Victorian home, a tenant whose rent will make it possible for them to afford the mortgage payment, encounter a well-dressed, professional looking man who answers their ad. Accepting his very believable story, they rent to him without checking any of the information he gives them.

A series of peculiar events, however, reveals a psychopathic individual who refuses to pay the rent, does great damage to the apartment, drives the other tenants out, and resists the owners' every attempt to evict him—even to the point of obtaining a court order preventing the owners from coming near him. Had they checked his references, the owners find out later, they could have avoided this nightmare.

While exaggerated in the movie, the risks assumed by a landlord are very real. No matter how nice a tenant seems, a well-designed application form and a thorough background check are essential. The best tenants will exhibit the following important characteristics, all of which can be verified:

- *Secure employment:* The best tenants will have been at their present job for several years; they earn sufficient income to cover the rent, utilities, and other living expenses; and there is every reason to believe they will continue to be employed.

- *Longevity:* The best tenants have a history of staying put. They do not move around a lot.

- *Clean:* The ideal tenant keeps the apartment clean and well-maintained, and takes responsibility for keeping the common areas clean.

- *Quiet:* The ideal tenant does not cause disturbances around the building.

- *Reliable:* The best tenant has a history of paying bills on time, particularly the rent. If the background check indicates that the new tenant passes muster, a carefully prepared lease form spells out the terms and seals the agreement with the tenant. The only thing left: to move the new tenant into their new home.

# Chapter

# 8

# Lease Application Forms

I f your sales presentation has been successful, the prospective tenant will fill out an application form and leave it, along with an application fee and a deposit to hold the apartment. The form you use should ask for enough information so that you can perform a thorough background check. Commercially prepared application forms are available through stationery and office supply stores, or you can prepare your own. Figure 8–1 is a sample application form that can be copied for your use.

## Important Sections

No matter which form you use, be certain that the following sections are included and are filled out completely by the applicant:

- *Names.* The form should include the name of the applicant, (both husband and wife, if married), plus the names of any other persons who are planning to live in the apartment. Later, all of these names will appear on the lease. If two or more

## Figure 8–1: Lease Application Form Front Page

—— **APPLICATION FOR LEASE** ——

DATE: _____ APPLICATION FOR: _____ APT _____ OCCUPANCY DATE: _____

RENT AMOUNT: $_____ SECURITY DEPOSIT AMOUNT: $_____ NON-REFUNDABLE $25.00 CREDIT CHECK RECD: _____ DEPOSIT RECD: $_____

APPLICANT _____ AGE _____ SPOUSE _____ AGE _____

BIRTH DATE _____ SOC. SEC. # _____ BIRTH DATE _____ SOC. SEC. # _____

DRIVER'S LICENSE # _____ DRIVER'S LICENSE # _____

CURRENT EMPLOYER _____ CURRENT EMPLOYER _____

ADDRESS _____ PHONE _____ ADDRESS _____ PHONE _____

CONTACT PERSON _____ CONTACT PERSON _____

POSITION _____ YRS SERVICE _____ POSITION _____ YRS SERVICE _____

WEEKLY PAY $ _____ MONTHLY PAY $ _____ WEEKLY PAY $ _____ MONTHLY PAY $ _____

CURRENT ADDRESS _____ CITY _____ ZIP _____ PHONE_____

LANDLORD NAME _____ PHONE_____ HOW LONG?_____

PREVIOUS ADDRESS _____ CITY _____ ZIP _____ PHONE_____

LANDLORD NAME _____ PHONE_____ HOW LONG?_____

WELFARE ASSISTANCE ONLY: ☐ AFDC  ☐ GENERAL ASSISTANCE  ☐ AID TO THE ELDERLY    MONTHLY INCOME: $_____

CASE WORKER: _____ OFFICE LOCATION: _____ PHONE: _____

| CREDIT ACCOUNTS: | | NAMES OF CHILDREN AND OTHER TENANTS: | | |
|---|---|---|---|---|
| 1._____ | # _____ | 1. Name _____ | Age _____ | Sex _____ |
| 2._____ | # _____ | 2.Name _____ | Age _____ | Sex _____ |
| 3._____ | # _____ | 3. Name _____ | Age _____ | Sex _____ |
| 4._____ | # _____ | 4.Name _____ | Age _____ | Sex _____ |

CHECKING ACCT AT: _____ # _____ HOW LONG?_____

SAVINGS ACCT AT: _____ # _____ HOW LONG?_____

CAR MAKE _____ YEAR _____ LICENSE NO. _____ FINANCED BY _____

CAR MAKE _____ YEAR _____ LICENSE NO. _____ FINANCED BY _____

ADDITIONAL REFERENCES:

NAME _____ RELATIONSHIP _____ PHONE _____

NAME _____ RELATIONSHIP _____ PHONE _____

IN EMERGENCY NOTIFY_____ RELATIONSHIP _____ PHONE _____

ADDRESS _____ CITY_____

I represent to you that I have read this entire application and that all of the above information hereon is true and correct. I further represent that my rental and credit records are in good standing with no judgments or liens against me. If any of the above information is false, I hereby agree that my entire deposit may be forfeited to you. I also agree that if I am accepted and fail to complete this transaction by signing your lease, my entire deposit will be forfeited to you. I understand that my $25.00 credit check fee is nonrefundable. I also understand that this is not a lease and should my application be accepted, I agree to sign your lease form currently in use. If for any reason whatsoever you are unable to make the apartment which is the subject of this application available at the beginning of the lease term, I hereby waive any and all rights to seek to recover any damages whatsoever against you, including without limitation, actual, punitive or consequential damages. IT IS POLICY NOT TO DISCRIMINATE RENTALS ON THE BASIS OF RACE, CREED, COLOR, NATIONAL ORIGIN, RELIGION, AGE OR SEX.

_____    _____

APPLICANT                                    DATE

_____    _____

APPLICANT                                    DATE

# Figure 8-1: Lease Application Form Back Page

*This is a legal document that imposes legal obligation on you and may under some circumstances result in forfeiture of your earnest money. Please read carefully.*

## AUTHORIZATION TO CHECK CREDIT

*In connection with your apartment application a consumer or credit reporting agency may be asked to make an investigative consumer or credit report on you.*

**Credit Check:** By signing below, I (we) hereby authorize agent and any consumer or credit reporting agency or bureau employed by it to investigate my (our) character, general reputation, mode of living, and credit and financial responsibility as well as the statements made in this application. I (we) also authorize such credit or consumer reporting agency or bureau to make a consumer or credit report available to the agent. I understand there is a charge of $25.00 for this service and that this charge is non-refundable.

## AGREEMENT

I (we) hereby request the owner of the apartment described on the reverse side of this document to lease the same to me (us) for the term indicated, and offer to pay for this apartment the indicated monthly rent. All statements by me (us) that appear on the application are true.

This proposal and application shall remain open for a period of ten days from this date, and shall become binding upon the owner only when accepted by him or his agent. Acceptance will be indicated by the completion of a suitable lease form, signed by me (us) and the owner or his authorized agent.

I (we) deposit $_____ as earnest money with agent. This deposit will be refunded to me if this proposal or my stated references and credit history are not satisfactory to the owner. If the proposal is accepted, this deposit will be applied toward a security deposit of $_____.

I (we) agree to execute a written lease, if requested, for the apartment according to the terms on the reverse, and at the same time to pay the balance of the first month's rent. If this application is accepted by the owner or his agent, and I refuse or fail to execute the lease as requested, or to pay the balance due, this deposit may be retained by the agent in payment for services provided in taking this application and investigating my references.

I (we) understand all rent is due and payable in advance on the first day of each month.

**Pets:** I (we) understand that no dog, cat or any other animal is to be kept on the premises without express written permission of the owner.

| | |
|---|---|
| APPLICANT | DATE |
| APPLICANT | DATE |

individuals who are not married are planning to share the apartment, obtain an application from each of them.

- *Social Security number.* Each adult who is living in the apartment must provide a Social Security number. This is essential for completing a credit check.

- *Driver's license number.* This number will not be used during the background check, but it is information that may be used later for identification purposes in the unlikely event that a collection agency must be employed to collect past-due rents after a tenant has left the building (Chapter 14).

- *Current employer.* Do not accept an applicant's word that he or she is employed. Obtain the name, phone number, address, and immediate supervisor of the applicant's employer. Also find out how many years the applicant has worked there, the weekly or monthly pay, and the position with the company.

- *Previous addresses.* Find out where the applicant has lived during the past five years. Find out the name of the landlord and the landlord's phone number, as well as how long they lived at each address.

- *Credit accounts.* Find out where the applicant has outstanding credit. Although you will not be checking each of these accounts (this will be done by the professional credit check company), this information is helpful in defining the overall profile of the applicant. It also lets the applicant know that you are serious about checking his or her background.

- *Bank accounts.* Find out where the applicant has a checking and savings account.

- *Automobiles.* Find out how many automobiles the applicant owns, the year, the make, the model and the license plate number. Again this helps fill out the profile and may, at some time, provide important identifying information.

- *Alternate sources of income:* If an applicant is not employed, but has an alternate source of income (Social Security, investment income, etc.) that may be adequate to cover the rent, find out what that income is, along with some means of verifying it.

- *References.* Obtain at least two names of people who can provide references for the applicant. Although they probably will not be contacted, providing the names encourages the tenant to believe that you are serious about the background check.

- *Authorization to check credit.* Be certain to include a section that authorizes you to check the applicant's credit. If the form does not include this section, add it to the form or attach it as a second page. A credit check must not be done without authorization; doing so exposes the landlord to legal action.

- *Application fee.* Be sure to explain to the applicant that you will charge an application fee, which covers the cost of the credit check and the background search. This fee can be whatever amount you decide. It is common for management firms to charge anywhere from $15 to $30. Explain to the applicant that the application fee is non-refundable. Even if you reject the application, the fee will not be returned to them.

- *Earnest money deposit.* If the applicant definitely wants the apartment, require an earnest money deposit, which gives them first right to the apartment if their application is approved. The earnest money deposit should be the equivalent of one month's rent, or some lesser amount if acceptable, but no less than $100. The applicant should understand that the deposit will not be refunded if they cancel their application. It will be refunded, however, if the application is not approved.

Be certain the applicant knows that all information on the application form will be verified. Explain that if they know of some problem with their credit, or if any of the information can not be verified, the application will be rejected and they will lose their application fee.

Once the applicant has been so advised and wishes to proceed, accept the application and the fee (along with the deposit, if any) and proceed with the background check.

# Chapter

# 9

# Approving the Application

**W**ith application and check in hand, the temptation is to hurry through the approval process—or to ignore it altogether. That would be a big mistake. Take the time to conduct a thorough background check before approving an application. Sometimes the nicest of applicants have skeletons in the closet that you should know about. It costs nothing to reject an application based on a poor credit history or a previous eviction. Once you sign a lease and accept money from the applicant, however, it could cost plenty if the applicant turns out to be a bad risk.

You can check the applicant's background yourself or hire a company to do it for you. For a fee, a number of companies will produce a comprehensive report, including an applicant's credit history, verification of employment, and a report from previous landlords. Or you can do most of the work yourself, except the credit history, which must be produced by an authorized company. Either way, each part must be done well to produce a substantive report.

## Credit History

There are several companies that will produce a report of an applicant's credit history. To complete the credit check, the companies must have the applicant's social security number and present address. A credit check can be produced and faxed to you almost immediately. By mail it takes a little longer. If you have a computer and a modem, you can produce the credit check yourself at a very low cost through one of the major credit rating companies.

## Verification of Employment

Call the employer to verify employment. Most employers will not reveal the actual amount the applicant earns, but will verify the length of time the applicant has been employed with them. Ask whether the employer is happy with the applicant's performance, and whether the applicant is a reliable employee. Listen for subtle indicators of displeasure. It is important to know how secure the employment is. If you are managing a building with a large percentage of high risk applicants, also ask the applicant for two recent pay stubs and a picture identification (to verify that the pay stubs belong to the applicant). Applicants have been know to list false employment information, using a friend or relative to verify a non-existent job.

## Talk to the Present Landlord

Talk to the applicant's landlord yourself. These are the questions to ask:

"Does (applicant's name) presently rent an apartment (or house) from you?"

"How long have they lived there?"

"How many times during the past year were they late in paying their rent?"

"Would you rent to them again?"

"Why have they chosen to move?"

Most landlords will be honest in answering these questions, particularly if the tenant has not been a problem. If a tenant has been particularly difficult, however, the landlord may not be truthful, realizing that if you decline to rent to the applicant he or she will be stuck with them. For that reason, the most honest report usually comes from the previous landlord, who has nothing to lose from being honest.

## Prior Landlord

If the applicant has not lived at the present address for at least two years, talk with the prior landlord. Ask the same questions that were asked of the present landlord. The prior landlord, having no ulterior motive, will usually be more honest than the first.

## Verify Alternative Sources of Income

If the applicant depends upon Social Security, disability pay, welfare, investment income, or some other alternative source of income, request an award letter or the two most recent checkstubs to verify the income.

## Self-Employed Applicants

If an applicant is self-employed, ask to see copies of his or her latest tax returns to verify employment. Otherwise, ask for a financial statement that has been verified by the applicant's bank.

## How Much Income Should the Applicant Earn?

Some management firms use elaborate tables to determine how much rent an applicant can afford. A simpler rule-of-thumb method is to total the applicant's monthly obligations including the rent. If that total exceeds 40 percent of the applicant's income, be careful. If the applicant has a strong credit history and rental history, take the risk. If there have been any problems in the past, however, reject the application.

# Decision Making: The Three-Strike Rule

When the background check is complete and a decision must be made, think of each of the following as a strike against the candidate:

- *Strike 1:* If the applicant is unemployed, even if there are alternative sources of income. If an applicant indicates that he or she is self-employed, demand verification. Without verification, reject the assertion.

- *Strike 2:* Poor credit history. Any credit problem at all should be considered strike two.

- *Strike 3:* No previous landlord. If the applicant indicates that he or she lives with parents, other family members or a friend. Or if no prior landlord can be contacted, consider that strike three.

If an applicant strikes out, reject the application.

If the applicant has two strikes but the third area is strong, the application probably should be rejected, but you might consider the present situation: are there verifiable circumstances that led to a poor report and have steps been taken to protect against it happening again? Is there a strong co-signer? Is the applicant able to increase the security deposit significantly?

If the applicant suffers from one strike, but the other two areas are strong, consider the application but be careful to ascertain why the situation exists.

The best tenant, of course, will have no strikes. Unfortunately, it is not always possible to find the best tenant, and some compromises have to be made. Take steps like the above, however, to make sure that any such compromises do not produce bad outcomes.

# Chapter

# 10

# How to Prepare an
# Apartment Lease

A written lease is not required to rent an apartment; an oral agreement is sufficient to establish legal tenancy. Many landlords prefer not to use written leases on the assumption that they provide more protection for the tenant than the landlord. A well-written lease, however, provides important protection for both the tenant and the landlord. More important, a carefully worded lease establishes clear expectations for the tenant and can lead to fewer conflicts than an oral agreement.

## Commercial Lease Forms

Most stationery stores sell commercially produced lease forms. These forms have been prepared by qualified real estate attorneys and have been modified through the years to reflect changing laws and regulations. The best of these forms are available through the local real estate board or the National Association of Realtors® in Chicago.

A lease is a contract between a landlord and a tenant. As such, it can include any terms and obligations that either party deems important. In most cases, the standard lease form does not include all of the conditions that the landlord may feel are important. In that case, the form typically allows space for additional covenants to be added (Figure 10–1).

# Lease Covenants That Are Prohibited by Law

Local ordinances and state laws often specifically prohibit a landlord from including certain agreements in a lease. If these agreements are included they are unenforceable, but do not invalidate the remainder of the lease as long as the lease includes a specific clause to that effect. Such prohibited provisions may include the following:

1. Any agreement that places a limit on the liability of the landlord as the result of willful misconduct or negligence.

2. Any clause that waives rights or remedies specifically granted by law.

3. Any agreement to waive attorney's fees or for either party to pay the other's attorney's fees, unless the law requires it.

# Lease Riders

An attachment to a lease form that adds additional agreements or covers specific situations is called a lease rider. When a lease rider is used, the lease form itself must indicate the existence of the lease rider, and the lease rider must include specific language that makes it a part of the lease agreement.

## Additional Covenants Rider

If the list of additional covenants to be added to a standard lease form exceeds the available space, use a lease rider to add them to the lease (Figure 10.2).

## Figure 10–1: Apartment Lease

UNIVERSITY PRINTING COMPANY
CHICAGO, IL

**NO. 15**

# APARTMENT LEASE
### NOT FURNISHED

©CHICAGO BOARD OF REALTORS®
COPYRIGHT 1990
ALL RIGHTS RESERVED

| DATE OF LEASE | TERM OF LEASE | | MONTHLY RENT | SECURITY DEPOSIT* |
|---|---|---|---|---|
| | BEGINNING | ENDING | | |
| April 22, 1992 | May 1, 1992 | April 30, 1993 | $650.00 | $650.00 |

**ADDITIONAL CHARGES AND FEES**

| | | | Deposit $65.00 | |
|---|---|---|---|---|
| Late Charge $ 25.00 | Returned Check Charge $ 25 | Reletting Charge $ 200 | Parking Fee $ $65.00 | Laundry Room Fee $ -0- |
| Social Security No. 123-45-6789 | Storage Fee $ -0- | | $ | |

*"IF NONE, WRITE "NONE." Paragraph 5 of Lease Agreements and Covenants then INAPPLICABLE.*

(Owner or agent authorized
to manage the Apartment)

**TENANT**

TENANT • Herbert Fall

APARTMENT • 3B

BUILDING • 4567 Spring Court

CITY • Chicago, IL 60000

**LESSOR**

NAME • John Winters
Winters Property Management

ADDRESS • 1011 Summer Lane

CITY • Chicago, IL 60000

PHONE • 555-4488

In consideration of the mutual agreements and covenants set forth below and on the reverse side hereof (the same being fully included as part of this Lease) Lessor hereby leases to Tenant and Tenant hereby leases from Lessor for use in accordance with paragraph 8 hereof the Apartment designated above, together with the fixtures and accessories belonging thereto, for the above Term. All parties listed above as Lessor and Tenant are herein referred to individually and collectively as Lessor and Tenant respectively.

**ADDITIONAL AGREEMENTS AND COVENANTS (including DECORATING AND REPAIRS), if any.**

See New Lease Rider for additional covenants.
Attached:
Building Rules Rider
Security Deposit Rider
Pet Rider
Tenant is assigned Garage space #4. See attached Rider.

**TENANT(S)**      **SIGNATURES**      **LESSOR(S)**

_____(SEAL)      _____(SEAL)

_____(SEAL)      _____(SEAL)

### LEASE AGREEMENTS AND COVENANTS

[Two columns of fine print lease terms, paragraphs 1 through 11, including: 1. RENT; 2. POSSESSION; 3. APPLICATION; 4. PROMISES OF THE PARTIES; 5. SECURITY DEPOSIT; 6. LESSOR TO MAINTAIN; 7. UTILITIES; 8. TENANT'S USE OF APARTMENT; 9. TENANT'S UPKEEP; 10. ALTERATIONS, ADDITIONS, FIXTURES, APPLIANCES, PERSONAL PROPERTY; 11. ACCESS.]

## Figure 10–2: New Lease Rider

This rider becomes a part of and is attached to the lease dated April 22, 1992, by and between John Winters (Lessor) and Herbert Fall (Lessee), covering the premises at 4567 Spring Court Apt. 3B, Chicago IL 60000.

To the extent of any conflict in terms, the terms and conditions of this rider shall govern over the terms and conditions of the aforesaid lease.

Additional covenants of the lease are as follows:

27. Maximum occupancy of this apartment is 2. Apartment is rented to above listed tenant(s) only. An additional charge of $10.00 per day will be assessed for any other person living in apartment longer than 10 days.

28. Rent is due on the 1st of each month. A late charge of $25.00 will be assessed when rent is received later than the 10th of the month.

29. Tenant is responsible for providing electricity and cooking gas.

30. Tenant acknowledges working smoke detector, and is responsible for changing battery.

31. No pets are allowed without written consent of owner.

32. In the event tenant leaves apartment before the lease expiration date and the apartment is rerented, a reletting fee of $200.00 will be charged.

33. Security deposits may not be used as rent payments. When tenant vacates apartment at the end of the lease, the security deposit may not be used as the last month's rent.

34. Apartment is to be left in a clean condition. If cleaning is necessary after apartment is vacated, tenant will be charged for the costs.

35. Tenant agrees to give Lessor a minimum of 30 days written notice if apartment is to be vacated at the end of the lease period. Security deposits will be returned by mail within 30 days of vacating, subject to any costs associated with cleaning or repairing apartment.

36. Tenant agrees to notify utility companies promptly of new address and move-in date.

37. Tenant acknowledges stove and refrigerator are furnished with the apartment and are the property of the building owner. Damage caused to either appliance by improper operation is the responsibility of the tenant.

Dated: April 22, 1992.

LESSEE:                                          LESSOR:

_____                 _____
Herbert Fall                                     John Winters
                                                 Winters Property Management

## Appliance Provision

If the landlord provides the appliances for the apartment, it should be specifically stipulated in the lease. Without such specific language, the landlord often has no recourse if tenants take one or more of the appliances when they leave. Likewise, if tenants choose to use their own appliances the lease should state that fact by including it in the additional covenants.

## Lease Riders for High Risk Properties

Figure 10–3 is a list of additional covenants for a building that serves a higher risk group of tenants. These covenants spell out certain tenant obligations and provide specific recourse for the landlord so that problematic tenants can be dealt with quickly and effectively. Be careful that any added provisions are not prohibited by local ordinances or state laws.

### Pet Rider

You may decide not to allow any tenants to keep pets. This is your right. Most standard lease forms specify that no pets are allowed unless specific permission has been granted by the landlord. In some buildings, however, you may decide that pets are okay as long as you have recourse in the event the pet becomes a nuisance. One way to protect yourself is to use a pet rider (Figure 10–4) and to charge an additional amount on the security deposit. If the tenants have no pet when they move in, but decide to obtain a pet later, complete a pet rider at that time. The pet rider can be added at any time during the term of the lease.

### Garage Rider

When a property offers garage spaces, off-street parking or carports to tenants at an additional cost, a specific rider should be attached to the lease indicating the terms and conditions of the rental agreement. The lease form itself should note the additional rent and the additional deposit, if any, that are required. In addition, the rider should also specify the deposit and the monthly rent that is being charged for the parking space (Figure 10–5). The tenant should fill out a specific infor-

# Figure 10–3: Building Rules Lease Rider

This rider becomes a part of and is attached to the lease dated April 22, 1992, by and between John Winters (Lessor) and Herbert Fall (Lessee), covering the premises at 4567 Spring Court Apt. 3B, Chicago IL 60000.

To the extent of any conflict in terms, the terms and conditions of this rider shall govern over the terms and conditions of the aforesaid lease.

1. All moving of furniture in and out of the building must be done through the rear stairway. Please do not move in or out through the front stairway. Tenants ignoring this rule are subject to charges for damage to the hallways.

2. Tenants are advised to obtain renter's insurance, which will provide protection in the case of fire, theft or water damage to the apartment.

3. Tenants are required to place all trash and refuse INSIDE the designated containers.

4. Pets must be taken in and out the rear stairway, and must be taken off the grounds for toileting. If a pet makes a mess in or around the building, the tenant must clean up the mess immediately. Pets are to be supervised at all times. In common areas, pets must be leashed and kept quiet. Loud barking at any time is not permitted.

5. Drug use will not be tolerated in or around the building. The lease of any tenant involved in the use, trafficking, storing, purchasing, selling, or manufacturing of any controlled substance within their apartment, in the common areas of the building, or in the area surrounding the building will be terminated, and eviction proceedings will begin immediately.

6. Gang activity will not be tolerated in or around the building. Tenants sporting gang paraphernalia (dress, caps, colors, etc.) will be subject to eviction. Parents are responsible for their children's activities and actions and that of their children's guests. Parents are to ensure that their children are not involved in gang activities. Failure to do so will result in immediate termination of the lease.

7. No loitering will be tolerated in or around the building. The term "loitering" refers to, but is not limited to, sitting in chairs in the front of the building, sitting on cars parked in front of or to the side of the building, congregating in the courtyards, gangways, parkways or on the sidewalk in front of the building or in the alleys behind the building.

8. No loud noise will be tolerated in or around the building. Loud noises include, but are not limited to, stereos, radios, televisions and musical instruments played too loudly, loud conversation, yelling, loud mufflers on cars, honking horns, etc. Please do not allow any loud noise disrupt other tenants' or neighbors' peaceful enjoyment of their homes.

9. Tenants are responsible for keeping their apartments in good, clean condition through regular cleaning and by avoiding activities that will damage the floors and walls. Tenants should notify the janitor to correct any plumbing or electrical problems, and to correct any problems in the common areas (e.g., broken lock, broken mailbox lock, burned-out light bulbs).

## Figure 10–3: Building Rules Lease Rider – Page 2

10. Children are not allowed to play in the common areas of the building (hallways, lobbies, courtyard, gangways, front and rear stairwells, parkways, or basement). Children are not to swing in trees or ride bicycles in the common areas (or on sidewalks or in parkways, in compliance with city ordinances relating to bicycle traffic). Children must not infringe on the rights of other tenants or neighbors to enjoy peace and tranquility in their homes, yards and common areas.

Children are to be supervised by an adult who is responsible for their actions at all times both inside and outside of the apartment. Parents or designated guardians are responsible for their children's actions and the actions of their children's guests. Parents or designated guardians will be held responsible (financially and otherwise) for any damage caused by their children to the building property, other tenants' personal property or the property of neighbors.

Parents or designated guardians are responsible for enforcing curfew and truancy laws, in accordance with city ordinances.

11. Barbecuing is permitted only on concrete surfaces as designated. No barbecue grills are allowed to be stored or used on wooden porches. After cooling, all barbecue grills must be stored inside the apartment or in a designated storage area. Tenants are required to dispose of all coals properly. Hot coals must not be dumped in the trash container or loosely in the alley. Coals must be allowed to cool thoroughly, then placed in plastic bags and disposed of with the trash. Do not deposit coals in or around the common areas, the lawn or the sidewalk.

12. Trash and garbage must be removed regularly from the apartment and placed in the trash containers that are provided. If there is no room in the container, do not leave trash on the ground. Notify the janitor if insufficient containers are available. Please do not litter the common areas, the parkways and sidewalks, laundry rooms, etc.

Dated April 22, 1992.

LESSEE:                                          LESSOR:

_____          _____
Herbert Fall                                     John Winters
                                                 Winters   Property   Management

## Figure 10–4: Pet Rider

LESSEE:        Herbert Fall                                          $ _50.00_ pet deposit
                             4567 Spring Court Apt. 3B
                             Chicago IL 60000

This rider becomes a part of and is attached to the lease dated April 22, 1992, by and between John Winters (Lessor) and Herbert Fall (Lessee), covering the premises at 4567 Spring Court Apt. 3B, Chicago IL 60000.

To the extent of any conflict in terms, the terms and conditions of this rider shall govern over the terms and conditions of the aforesaid lease.

In consideration of the sum of $50.00 pet deposit and in consideration of the mutual agreements and covenants set forth below, Lessor hereby permits Lessee to keep the following pet, hereinafter referred to as Pet, on the Premises for the term of the lease, and so long as Lessee is not in default of same.

Description: Type_____

Pounds_____ Breed_____ Color_____

1. Lessee agrees to clean up after the pet at all times on the Premises, in all common areas as well as in all areas of the building in which the Premises are situated.

2. Lessee shall keep the Pet quiet at all times.

3. Lessee agrees that the Pet shall not be taken outside the Premises, (including on the patio or balcony), unless the Pet is on a leash. The Pet shall be walked only in the area(s) so designated by Lessor from time to time.

4. Lessee agrees that in the event of any violation of the terms and conditions set forth above, the Lessor shall have the right to demand removal of the Pet from the Premises. Any refusal by Lessee to immediately comply with such demand shall be material breach of the lease, in which event Lessee shall forfeit to Lessor the aforementioned pet deposit and Lessor shall be entitled to any and all other remedies provided by law or equity. However, if Lessee removes the Pet upon such demand, the pet deposit shall be returned less damages, if any, to the Premises or the building or to the common areas where the Premises are situated, and said Lease shall continue in effect, except that this Rider shall be deemed null and void.

Dated: April 22, 1992

LESSEE:                                            LESSOR:

_____        _____

Herbert Fall                                        John Winters
                                                  Winters Property Management

## Figure 10–5: Garage or Parking Rider

LESSEE:            Herbert Fall                        $ __65.00__  deposit
                           4567 Spring Court Apt. 3B          $ __65.00__  monthly rent
                           Chicago IL 60000

This rider becomes a part of and is attached to the lease dated April 22, 1992, by and between John Winters (Lessor) and Herbert Fall (Lessee), covering the premises at 4567 Spring Court Apt. 3B, Chicago IL 60000.

To the extent of any conflict in terms, the terms and conditions of this rider shall govern over the terms and conditions of the aforesaid lease.

In consideration of the deposit of the sum of $65.00 and in consideration of the mutual agreements and covenants set forth below, Lessor hereby leases to Lessee Garage space #4 at the above address.

1. Lessee agrees to maintain the space(s) in a clean and sanitary condition at all times.

2. Lessee agrees to utilize the space(s) only for the purpose of parking the assigned vehicle(s).

3. Lessee agrees to remove any vehicle deemed by Lessor to be unsightly or in non-working condition within five (5) days of notification.

4. Lessee agrees that in the event of any violation of the terms and conditions set forth above, the Lessor shall have the right to make a demand for immediate possession of said space(s). Any refusal by Lessee to comply with such demand by Lessor to return said space(s) shall be material breach of the lease, and Lessor shall be entitled to retain aforementioned deposit as well as be entitled to any and all other remedies provided by law or equity. However, if Lessee returns said space(s) upon such demand, the deposit shall be returned less damages, if any, caused by violation hereof and said Lease shall continue in effect, except that this Rider shall be deemed null and void.

Dated:  April 22, 1992

LESSEE:                                               LESSOR:

_____        _____

Herbert Fall                                   John Winters
                                                 Winters Property Management

mation form covering the vehicle or vehicles that will be using the space (Figure 10–6).

## Security Deposit Agreement

One of the most common sources of disagreement and friction between tenants and landlords is the security deposit. Landlords who refuse to return security deposits, tenants who assume they can apply the security to the last month's rent, landlords who retain a portion or all of the deposit to cover cleaning or repairs that in fact were nothing more than normal wear and tear: these are all possible points of dispute.

It is impossible, unfortunately, to eliminate all such conflict. Nevertheless, a security deposit agreement (Figure 10–7) that is signed by both parties serves to establish, from the beginning, the conditions under which a deposit will be held, the conditions under which the deposit will be returned or not returned, and the expectations on the part of the landlord regarding the application of the deposit toward the tenant's rent obligations.

The security deposit agreement should also include a list of specific charges that will be assessed if the apartment is left in an unsatisfactory condition. Such a list serves two purposes: first, in the event that repairs or cleaning are necessary when the tenant moves out, it is easy to determine how much to charge. Second, when a tenant knows that certain items will be charged against the security deposit, they have a tendency to leave the apartment in better condition. This makes it much easier and less costly to prepare the apartment for the next tenant.

## Lease Renewal Rider

When it comes time to renew a lease, a simple and inexpensive way to extend the existing lease is through a lease renewal rider (Figure 10–8). This rider, which like other riders must include specific language attaching it to the original lease, allows the landlord to extend the period of the lease, change the amount of the rent, change the amount of the security deposit, and modify the original lease without drafting an entirely new lease form. Usually only one page in length, the lease renewal form is simple and easy to handle through the mail,

## Figure 10–6: Application for Parking or Garage Space

---

### APPLICATION FOR PARKING OR GARAGE SPACE

NAME_____ APT_____

ADDRESS_____

TELEPHONE (HOME)_____ (BUSINESS)_____

MAKE OF CAR_____ MODEL_____ COLOR_____

D.L. NUMBER_____

LICENSE PLATE_____ STATE_____

ASSIGNED SPACE NUMBER_____

---

and reassures the tenant that nothing material is being altered regarding the original lease agreement.

As with the lease itself, the terms and conditions of the lease renewal rider are subject to the needs of the landlord and the specific circumstances of the lease. Any terms and agreements may be included that are mutually acceptable between the tenant and the landlord as long as they do not violate local or state ordinances or rules of law.

### *Lease Cancellation Rider*

A tenant who anticipates not being able to complete the full term of a lease because of certain circumstances—an impending job transfer, for example, or plans to purchase a home—should complete a lease cancellation rider (Figure 10–9), which spells out the terms and conditions under which the lease will be terminated early.

## Figure 10–7: Security Deposit Agreement

LESSEE:        Herbert Fall
                        4567 Spring Court Apt. 3B
                        Chicago IL 60000

This rider becomes a part of and is attached to the lease dated April 22, 1992, by and between John Winters (Lessor) and Herbert Fall (Lessee), covering the premises at 4567 Spring Court Apt. 3B, Chicago IL 60000.

To the extent of any conflict in terms, the terms and conditions of this rider shall govern over the terms and conditions of the aforesaid lease.

LESSOR acknowledges receipt of $650.00 as security deposit for above named premises. This deposit will be refunded in full within 30 days after the expiration of this lease, if tenant has complied with the following provisions:

1. The full term of the lease has expired.

2. The entire apartment, including stove, refrigerator, other appliances, cabinets, closets, bathroom, carpet, floors, windows, light fixtures, balcony, etc. is clean.

3. No damage to the apartment other than that caused by normal wear and tear.

4. No scratches in the floor, no indentations in the floor.

5. Floor has been restored to original condition if carpet, linoleum or tile has been installed, unless installation has been approved by building owner.

6. No wallcoverings, unless installation has been approved by building owner.

7. No large holes in the walls; no scratches, stickers, or marks on the walls.

8. All trash and discarded items have been placed in approved trash containers.

9. Carpet has been professionally cleaned.

10. All keys (including mailbox keys) have been returned.

11. Tenant owes no late charges or delinquent rent.

12. Tenant has left forwarding address.

If any of these provisions have not been met satisfactorily, tenant will be charged according to the following cost schedule:

CLEANING, REPAIRING OR REPLACEMENT CHARGES

If the items listed below have not been left in a clean and working condition, the following charges will be deducted from the security deposit or must be paid to the owner if the security deposit is insufficient to cover the charges. These prices are based on minimum costs and may not cover the entire cost of cleaning or repairing an item. If the actual cost is higher, tenant will be responsible for paying the actual cost.

This is not necessarily a complete list. Tenant is subject to cleaning or repair charges in addition to those appearing on this list.

## Figure 10–7: Security Deposit Agreement, Page Two

**Cleaning**

Kitchen:

| | | | | | |
|---|---|---|---|---|---|
| Stove top | $20.00 | Oven | $30.00 | Vent hood | $15.00 |
| Refrigerator | $40.00 | Cabinets | $25.00 | Counter tops | $10.00 |

Bathroom:

| | | | | | |
|---|---|---|---|---|---|
| Toilet | $10.00 | Tub/shower | $20.00 | Med. cabinet | $5.00 |
| Vanity | $10.00 | Sink | $5.00 | | |

Miscellaneous:

| | | | | | |
|---|---|---|---|---|---|
| Carpet/room | $35.00 | Closets, ea. | $10.00 | Windows, ea. | $5.00 |

All other cleaning, including trash removal, cleaning floors, washing walls, vacuuming, etc. will be charged at an hourly rate of $15.00.

**Repairing**

Appliances: actual cost of repairs

Patching larger holes (1/2" to 2") ea.: $12.00

Excessive painting and decorating costs (i.e., priming, double coating, removing wall coverings): $20.00/hour plus cost of materials

Miscellaneous repairs (i.e., door locks, cabinet pulls, light fixtures): $20.00/hour plus cost of materials

**Replacement charges**

If any items are missing or damaged to the point that they must be replaced, tenant will pay to have them replaced. The following charges are based on minimum costs. Tenant is responsible for the entire cost of the item plus labor charges if the actual cost is higher than the minimum.

| | | | | | |
|---|---|---|---|---|---|
| Light bulbs, ea. | $1.50 | Window glass | $75.00 | Screens | $35.00 |
| Mailbox key | $25.00 | Door key, ea. | $25.00 | Ice tray, ea. | $3.00 |
| Refrig. shelves | $30.00 | Crisper cover | $30.00 | Stove knob | $5.00 |
| Burner pan, ea. | $10.00 | Light fixture | $75.00 | Mini-blind | $35.00 |
| Toilet seat | $25.00 | Window shade | $20.00 | | |

Tenant agrees that the costs as set out above are not unreasonable charges for the work or items described, and agrees to pay the owner either the minimum costs or the actual costs of all such work if higher than the minimum.

Dated: April 22, 1992.

LESSEE:                                         LESSOR:

_____                          _____

Herbert Fall                                    John Winters
                                                Winters Property Management

## Figure 10–8: Lease Renewal Rider

LESSEE:

Herbert Fall
4567 Spring Court Apt. 3B
Chicago IL 60000

This rider becomes a part of and is attached to the lease dated April 22, 1992, by and between John Winters (Lessor) and Herbert Fall (Lessee), covering the premises at 4567 Spring Court, Apt. 3B, Chicago IL 60000, and extends the term of the lease for a period of twelve months from May 1, 1993 to April 30, 1994.

The terms and conditions thereof shall remain in force with the following exceptions, if any:

The rent increases to $675.00 per month.

The new security deposit will be $675.00. This represents an increase of $25.00, which must be received by Lessor to make this rider valid.

Dated this _____ day of _____, 19____

LESSEE:                                        LESSOR:

_____                      _____
Herbert Fall                                   John Winters
                                               Winters Property Management

## Figure 10–9: Lease Cancellation Rider

LESSEE:   Herbert Fall
             4567 Spring Court Apt. 3B
             Chicago IL 60000

This rider becomes a part of and is attached to the lease dated April 22, 1992, by and between John Winters (Lessor) and Herbert Fall (Lessee), covering the premises at 4567 Spring Court Apt. 3B, Chicago IL 60000.

The terms and conditions of this rider shall govern over the terms and conditions of the attached lease agreement.

Lessee shall have the right to terminate this Lease on the last day of any calendar month during the term of the Lease, provided the following conditions are met:

1. Lessee must give Lessor not less than sixty (60) days prior written notice of intention to terminate Lease.

2. All rents and other charges are paid in full up to the intended cancellation.

3. Lessee is not in default of Lease terms and conditions.

4. Lessee shall pay Lessor $200 reletting fee, per lease conditions, said fee not to be taken from security deposit.


Dated this _____ day of _____, 199__

LESSEE:                                                  LESSOR:


_____                _____
Herbert Fall                                             John Winters
                                                 Winters Property Management

## Signing the Lease

When the lease is prepared and ready for signing, arrange to meet the new tenants at the apartment to sign the lease and to complete an inspection tour. All parties must be present to sign the appropriate forms and copies are retained by both parties. If a face-to-face meeting is not possible and the lease must be mailed, send the tenant two unsigned copies of the lease along with all riders and request that they sign and return both copies. Then sign both copies yourself and return one to the tenant. In no case should a landlord sign a lease prior to the tenant signing, particularly if the lease is to be mailed. The tenant may end up with a signed lease while the landlord has none.

# Chapter

# 11

# When It's Time for the New Tenant to Move In

**M**oving day establishes a business relationship between you and the tenant. If all is in order on that day, the tenant will move in with a feeling of appreciation as well as confidence in your ability to deliver on your obligations. If, on the other hand, the tenant encounters unfinished repairs, dirty appliances, a broken electric switch or a bathtub that will not drain, feelings of apprehension and disappointment likely will color your association for a long time.

Moving day is a difficult and stressful experience under the best of conditions. People's lives, which the day before were orderly and under control, are suddenly thrown upside down in a jumble of misplaced furniture, disorganized packing boxes, and a seemingly endless accumulation of odds and ends. How disappointing on top of that if the new tenant encounters keys that do not fit the locks, a carpet in need of shampooing, or a wall that remains unpainted.

The best of intentions means little when a tenant moves into an apartment that has not been suitably prepared. Coordinating the various workers to ready an apartment can be problematic. Nevertheless, on the day the new tenant is ready to move in, the apartment must be gleaming. Moving day establishes an attitude and a level of expectation. Be certain that the attitude is positive and the expectation is one of continued goodwill.

## A Four-Stage Move-In Process

### *Stage One: When the Lease Is Signed*

Preparation for a successful move-in begins the day the lease is signed. Meet the new tenants at the apartment to sign the lease, but before signing complete a tour of the apartment. Use a simple inspection form such as Figure 11–1 to note any minor damage that is not to be fixed (e.g., a chip in the bathroom sink, a small worn spot in the carpet, a scratch on the stove, windows where the tenant is to furnish the blinds). Note any items that have been left by a previous tenant (e.g., window blinds, wallpaper, a light fixture). Finally, list any repairs that are to be completed before move-in (e.g., dripping faucets, rooms to be painted, blinds to be installed, tile to be repaired).

If the apartment was properly prepared for showing (Chapter 5), very little will need to be done before move-in. If, however, the prospective tenants saw the apartment when it was still in the process of being prepared, or while the previous tenant still occupied it, the list of tasks to be completed before move-in day could be rather long. Some tasks, in fact, may not be completed until after move-in day, particularly if the time is short. Do not agree to any conditions that are unrealistic. If new mini-blinds normally require three weeks for delivery, establish a date for installation that allows plenty of time for delays. Better to exceed expectations by installing them before the agreed-upon date than to disappoint the new tenant by not meeting the deadline.

At the conclusion of the inspection tour both parties sign the form, which attaches as a rider to the lease. This inspection rider specifies the expected condition of the apartment on move-in day, as well as the condition in which the apartment is to be  left at the expiration of the lease.

# Figure 11–1: Tenant Inspection Form

Tenant Name _____
Apt. _____Building_____
Lease Date _____
Inspection Date _____

In each room, indicate items that need repair, items that have been left by previous tenants, items that are missing, and any minor damage that will not be repaired.

### LIVING ROOM

Walls and Ceiling _____
Floor_____
Baseboard and Trim_____
Doors_____
Windows_____
Closet_____
Electrical_____
Misc _____

### DINING ROOM

Walls and Ceiling _____
Floor_____
Baseboard and Trim_____
Doors_____
Windows_____
Closet_____
Electrical_____
Misc _____

### _____ BEDROOM

Walls and Ceiling _____
Floor_____
Baseboard and Trim_____
Doors_____
Windows_____
Closet_____
Electrical_____
Misc _____

### _____ BEDROOM

Walls and Ceiling _____
Floor_____
Baseboard and Trim_____
Doors_____
Windows_____
Closet_____
Electrical_____
Misc _____

### BATHROOM

Walls and Ceiling _____
Floor_____
Baseboard and Trim_____
Door _____
Window _____
Closet_____
Electrical_____
Plumbing_____
Fixtures_____
Misc _____

### KITCHEN

Walls and Ceiling _____
Floor_____
Baseboard and Trim_____
Doors_____
Windows_____
Closet_____
Cabinets _____
Plumbing _____
Appliances _____
Electrical _____

I have inspected the above apartment and am satisfied that all is in good order except the items noted.

Lessee:_____
Lessee:_____

## *Stage Two: A Few Days before Move-In*

- *Final Inspection:* When the workers have completed their jobs and the apartment is deemed ready for new tenants, complete a final inspection to establish whether the agreed-upon work has been done and that the quality of the work is satisfactory. This is the time to check locks and keys, to make sure the intercom is working, to check the stove and the refrigerator, to be sure the apartment is clean, that there is sufficient water pressure and that the drains all work efficiently. If any items remain undone, bring the workers back to finish them before move-in day. Reinspect the apartment after the workers have remedied the deficiencies. Do not be caught on move-in day by a tenant complaining that a drain is clogged, a blind doesn't work, a window won't open or a light does not turn on.

### Take Care of These Details

- *Keys:* Be certain the tenants will receive the appropriate keys. That may or may not include keys to the lobby, the front door, back door, extra deadbolt, mailbox, laundry room, basement, garage, etc. Different buildings employ different systems, but be certain the tenants receive every key they should have. Ascertain that each key fits the appropriate lock and that the lock works easily. Use WD40 on any sluggish locks that are encountered. When the keys have been checked, place them on a ring and tag them. The building should retain an extra set of keys, also tagged and hung in a safe place.

- *If the tenant wants new keys:* Tenants often want to change their locks after move-in, for security reasons. If they do, obtain copies of the new keys for the key box. To avoid huge rings of keys that open nothing, discard the old keys.

- *Utilities:* Gas and electric should be ready for use on the day the tenant moves in. They may want to heat up a pizza, wash their hands, or use hot water to wipe out the cabinets. How disappointing if the water is cold or the oven does not heat. If the utilities are turned on, determine whether they have been transferred into the tenant's name. If they remain in your name, you will be unfairly paying for the tenant's utilities.

- *Storage area:* Check the assigned storage room to be sure it has been cleaned out.

- *Elevator:* If a service elevator needs to be reserved, communicate this to the tenants in time for them to reserve a convenient block of time. A few days before move-in, confirm the tenant's reservation. If several tenants are moving in or out on one day, assign someone to monitor the use of the elevator so that no one extends past their allotted time period.

- *Mailbox and doorbell tags:* Place new name tags on the mail box and the door-bell directory on or before move-in day. If this task has been delegated, confirm that it will be completed. Check to be certain the spelling is correct and that the name tags look professional and are consistent with the other tags.

- *Welcoming letter:* On or before move-in day, deliver a welcoming letter to the new tenants (Figure 11–2). Include specific instructions, e.g., how to dispose of the debris that is left over from the move, where to dispose of trash and garbage, and how to contact the janitor (even though such information appears also on the lease). Include with the letter any of the following that seem important: instructions for operating appliances, laundry room instructions, change-of-address cards, a map of the area, an introduction to local community organizations, a bus and train schedule, and a list of important telephone numbers, i.e., police, fire, schools, restaurants, taxi companies, and public transportation agencies.

## Stage Three: Move-In Day

On move-in day meet the new tenants at the apartment. Walk through one last time to assure all parties that the apartment is in the

## Figure 11–2: Welcome Letter

April 30, 1992

Herbert Fall
4567 Spring Court Apt. 3B
Chicago IL 60000

Dear Mr. Fall:

Welcome to the Spring Court Apartments! I trust you will find your new home to be comfortable and your new neighbors to be hospitable. As you unpack, take notice of a few things:

Instructions for operating the stove and micro-wave can be found in the top left drawer in the kitchen. Please read them carefully and preserve them for future reference.

All the faucets and drains in the apartment have been checked, as have the lights and electrical outlets. If you experience any trouble, please call Mr. Hammer, the janitor, right away. His number is 555-6556.

The laundry room is located in the basement. Machines require $.75, in quarters only. Instructions for each of the machines are posted on the wall.

All trash should be place in the trash can just outside your back door. Mr. Hammer will take the trash to the dumpster twice a week, on Tuesday and Friday. If you have extra packing materials and debris left over from the move, please take it to the dumpster right away. It is located in the rear of the building, accessible from your back door and down the rear stairs.

The inter-com system is for your convenience and security. Please identify all callers before letting them in the vestibule door. If you do not know the caller, do not press the buzzer.

Bicycles may be stored in the first floor room. Please furnish your own chain and lock. We take no responsibility for the safety of your bike.

Because you are new to the neighborhood, here are some phone numbers you might find important:

| | | | |
|---|---|---|---|
| Police: | 555-2332 | Pizza (the best in the city): | 555-1119 |
| Fire: | 555-2333 | Drug Store: | 555-1232 |
| Taxi: | 555-9000 | Bus Company: | 555-7000 |

The Spring Court Apartments are a friendly place. I hope you make them your home for a long time.

With warm best wishes,

John Winters

condition that was agreed upon at the signing of the lease. Hand over the keys, show them the laundry facility, the storage area, the garage, and any parts of the building that they need to know about. Then get out of their hair; they have enough to think about without a landlord hovering about.

## Stage Four: The Follow-Up

A week or so after move-in day, contact the tenant by phone or in person to make sure that everything is in good working order.

## What to Do If One Tenant Is Moving In While Another Is Moving Out

When you find yourself in the enviable position of having a new tenant moving in on the day following the present tenant's departure, the four-stage process will be more difficult to implement. Try to schedule a few days between the moves, if possible, to complete any necessary work. If that is impossible, the work must be completed after the new tenant has moved in. If the outgoing tenant has received proper service during his or her residency, the apartment should have few problems in need of repair. If you have agreed to decorate the apartment, this should be scheduled at the new tenant's convenience, and the painters must be careful not to damage the tenant's furniture.

## What If Several Tenants Are Moving In and Out at the Same Time?

The four-stage process becomes even more problematic when several tenants are moving at the same time. What to do? As a guideline the four steps still have merit, but adjustments will need to be made to accommodate all of the tenants. Be creative, involve your employees, schedule the inspections at different times, be a problem-solver. The basis for the four-stage move-in process is to establish the right kind of business relationship and to ease the new tenants' transition into your building. Do whatever you need to do to accomplish that goal.

# Section

# III

# Handling Routine Operations

After the tenant has moved in, the tenant/landlord relationship settles into a series of routine operations. These operations include collecting the rent, renewing leases, and following up on minor repairs and other tenant needs. But all seemingly routine operations are much more than that. Each is a part of a business operation that should be focused on retaining the best tenants. If the tasks are handled well, the relationship between tenant and landlord—which was launched on a sea of goodwill—will continue to prosper. If not, the tenant will grow impatient and seek to live elsewhere.

# Chapter

# 12

## How to Keep
## the Best Tenants

In any business, retaining good customers is much less expensive than capturing new customers. So it is with the rental business. The costs associated with attracting the best tenants can be huge: advertising, redecorating, vacancies, not to mention the time spent showing the apartment. In addition, there is always the risk that a new tenant will not work out, which involves additional expense. Retention of a present tenant, on the other hand, involves satisfying that customer's needs which, if the building is well-managed on a day-to-day basis, is a reasonable undertaking.

Many landlords think nothing of painting, cleaning and repairing a vacant apartment to attract a new tenant, but are reluctant to redecorate an apartment or replace worn carpeting for a present tenant regardless of how long the tenant has lived in the apartment or how consistently they have paid the rent. This short-sighted attitude results in a much higher turn-over rate than is necessary. Good long-term tenants not only deserve some consideration, but doing so is good business.

# A Tenant Retention Plan

The best property managers and owners have a plan for retaining tenants. Unfortunately, such plans all too often involve little more than a monthly newsletter, a Christmas open house, or a policy to hire friendly receptionists. While such gimmicks are common in the field of property management, by themselves they are insufficient. The key to an effective tenant retention plan is not in the promotions, the parties or the gifts. The key to tenant retention is superior management. And superior management is grounded in a positive attitude toward tenants plus a systematic approach to keeping tenants satisfied.

The best tenants have a wide choice of living situations. Less desirable tenants—those with a poor credit history, a spotty work record, and an undesirable tenant history—are more limited in their choices of available housing. In the competition for the most desirable tenants, every landlord must ask the question, "What makes my apartments better than the competition?"

The truth is that the best tenants—and the best customers of any business—tend to stay with a business where they are treated as valued customers. Adding amenities, gimmicks and gadgets only goes so far—the competition can and will add those same gadgets, although bigger, better and newer. Tenants appreciate amenities, but more than the latest gadgets tenants want to live in a building where they are heard and their needs are responded to.

## *Attitudes*

The foundation of any good tenant retention plan is a customer-service attitude on the part of every person who works for the building. If you have a receptionist, that person must be customer-oriented, with an approach that conveys a sincere, caring attitude. But that part is obvious, and only goes so far. If the janitor responds with impatience to most repair orders, the best intentions of the dynamite receptionist will go for naught. From top to bottom, every person who works for the building must operate in a customer-service mode at all times. They must be accommodating, service oriented and friendly.

Do not fool yourself into keeping an irascible, foul-tempered janitor because "he knows everything about that old boiler." That same eccentric man is likely driving your best tenants into the arms of some other building manager whose employees make them feel cared for. When hiring a building manager, pay equal attention to their "people" skills and their management skills. Little good it does to have an efficiently operating building that is half full because the best tenants are fed up with being treated like wayward children.

Learn the names of your tenants, as well as the names of their children, and make sure your staff does the same. Address them by name when you see them. This kind of caring attitude leads to a sense of belonging and a sense of community, and that means far more than the latest model microwave oven.

### *Service*

The best attitudes are insufficient in the face of poor service. Rental customers are not just paying for a space in which to live. They are paying for, and have every right to expect, appropriate and timely service. Good service can be divided into two components: systems that work well consistently and prompt attention when the systems break down.

Basic systems should be well maintained and kept in good operating order. Those systems include the following:

- Adequate heat.

- All electrical devices in working order, including ceiling lights, wall switches, and outlets.

- Hot and cold water—under adequate pressure—in the bathrooms and kitchen.

- Sink drains and tub drains flow well.

- Stove and refrigerator (if provided) work well and do not have broken components.

- Air-conditioning, if furnished, is in good working condition.

- Lights in the common areas are always working.

- Doors and locks work properly.

## *Prompt Service*

Nothing the landlord does can prevent the periodic malfunctioning of any or all of the above systems. When something does go wrong, it is essential that the problem be promptly attended to. Just as you, yourself, are uncomfortable taking a cold shower, so is your tenant.

## *Clean, Safe, Quiet*

Nothing is as important to a good tenant as a quiet home, a clean environment, and a feeling of security. If any one of these three basic needs is missing, most of the good tenants will leave.

- *Clean:* Monitor the performance of your janitor and insist on a clean building at all times. If the janitor cannot perform up to your expectations, replace him or her, no matter how many children he or she has to feed.

- *Safe:* Do not allow loitering in or around the building. Make sure all outside doors close automatically and lock securely. Make sure the intercom system works well. Keep all lights in and around the building in good working order. Monitor the tenants and, after adequate warning, evict any who invite too many guests inside or who entertain unsavory guests, unsavory meaning anyone who, because of their looks or actions, appears to pose a threat to the safety and well-being of the other tenants.

   How many visitors are too many? Ultimately, it is up to the landlord to determine when the number of visitors exceeds a reasonable amount and constitutes a disruption for the other tenants. If there is a seemingly constant flow of visitors through an apartment, that is certainly too many. If reliable tenants are concerned about the number of people going in and out, that is too many. Before taking action, however, be sure to send a warning letter. If the warning letter is ineffective, follow up with a ten-day notice (Figure 18–2).

   Is there legal basis for eviction under such circumstances? A typical lease covenant reads, "Neither tenant nor any of these persons (guests) shall perform nor permit any practice that may damage the reputation of or otherwise be injurious to the building or neighborhood, or be disturbing to other tenants, be illegal, or increase the rate of insurance on the building." If that wording does not seem adequate, include a covenant in the lease rider that is more to the point, and which will become the basis of serving the ten-day notice. Use an attorney to help draft the appropriate language, and be careful not to violate the provisions of any state or local laws or ordinances.

- *Quiet:* After adequate warning, evict any tenants who cause unreasonable noise in the building. Monitor the tenants and remind them of the need to respect their neighbors' need for quiet.

### *Special Incentives*

In a competitive rental market, when most buildings are suffering a higher than normal vacancy rate (the competition for the best tenants is always fierce, regardless of overall economic conditions) special incentives, when accompanied by good customer service, can be effective in the retention of good tenants. One month free rent, a commonly used incentive in attracting new tenants, could also be used as an incentive to renew a lease. When the signed lease renewal rider is returned, the tenant receives a coupon that can be redeemed at the tenant's choice, perhaps during the Christmas season when bills are higher than usual. And consider returning the security deposit to a tenant who has been in the building for three years and compiled an excellent record.

# Communication

When a tenant places an angry call, it is often too late to regain a positive relationship. Typically, such calls come only after the tenant has fruitlessly attempted to remedy the situation by working with the janitor or the building manager, or has simply endured a series of relatively minor but cumulatively maddening problems. Open channels of communication prior to the blow-up might have avoided such a serious situation.

Many tenants, wishing to avoid confrontations, may never make a call. But when it comes time to renew the lease, they quietly allow the lease to expire and move to another building. Open lines of communication might have avoided such a loss. It is essential that tenants be heard, and the best way to assure open communication is through direct contact. Visit the building regularly at times when tenants are likely to be home. Many will see you and initiate contact. Introduce yourself to those you do not know and initiate a conversation. Call tenants periodically, new tenants within a few weeks of move-in, just to check on things. Once or twice a year, send a post-card requesting feedback from tenants. If circumstances justify, hold a tenant's meeting so that grievances can be aired.

## Inspections

An annual inspection of each tenant's apartment can uncover needed repairs (leaky faucets, cold radiators, etc.) as well as provide an opportunity to know what the tenant's needs and wishes are. When conducted with the right attitude (you are not checking up on the tenant—you are assuring good service) such a visit makes the tenant feel cared for. During such a visit, the tenant will often reveal what, if anything, will make it more likely that he or she will remain in the apartment. Within reason, acceding to such desires can pay off with a high rate of retention.

## Repairs Prior to Renewal

Sometime prior to lease renewal time, perhaps during your inspection visit, find something to repair in the apartment, something that has not been requested. Such a practice is consistent with the service orientation that is being developed and reinforces the tenant's feeling of being cared for. The repair can be as small as re-caulking the tub or tightening a loose doorknob.

## Renewal Incentives

Another effective practice is to offer renewal incentives in the form of upgrades in the apartment: a new light, perhaps, or re-tiling the kitchen floor. Always balance the cost of such incentives with the cost of attracting a new tenant. Will you have to tile the floor anyway if the tenant moves out? And you might have to repaint to boot.

## Employee Incentives

Because an effective tenant retention plan based on a customer-service orientation depends on the employees who are most often in contact with the tenants, consider implementing an incentive plan that rewards employees for a high rate of retention. The incentive can be monetary or might take another form: additional vacation days, a choose-your-own-gift catalog, a trip, etc. The purpose of such an incentive is to make it as important to the employees to retain as many tenants as possible, as it is to you. Therefore, work with the employee to choose an incentive that really works. Many times we mistakenly assume something will motivate another person when in fact it doesn't. If the other person has a role in choosing the incentive, it has a much greater chance to succeed.

# Chapter

# 13

# Collecting the Rents

If all other management responsibilities have been satisfied in a professional manner, collecting rents will not be a difficult task. Nevertheless, it is wise to establish a routine procedure for collecting rent, as well as a specific plan for enforcing payment. A rent collection policy should specify how and where the rent is to be paid, when the rent is due, and should establish the consequences for late payment and non-payment of rent.

## When Is the Rent Due?

Rent is due and payable on the first day of the month if so specified in the lease. If the lease period is different than a month, rent is due on the first day of the rental period. If the lease does not state clearly that rent is payable in advance, however, then the rent is due at the end of the rental period.

# Grace Period and Late Charges

When tenants do not pay the rent on time, a late charge can be assessed. This charge usually ranges from $10 to $25. More than $25 can be seen as excessive and may be challenged in court. Many municipalities have established limits on the amount of the late charge that can be assessed. In Chicago, for example, the limit is $10.

The grace period allowed before a late charge is assessed typically varies from five days to ten days, although a late fee may be assessed as early as the second day of the month. Generally, a more lenient policy that allows a grace period of ten days is recommended. Most tenants are familiar with business practices that allow such a period, and attempts to enforce a more strict policy can result in unnecessary feelings of resentment.

Some landlords feel that a late charge gives tenants license to pay late. Others feel the late charge is an effective incentive to pay on time. With most tenants, such a fee is an effective deterrent. When the grace period is exceeded, however, the late fee must be charged. If you feel the need for a further deterrent, allow only a limited number of late fees during the period of the lease. Such a policy would state that if a tenant incurs more than __X__ late charges (whatever number you decide) during the lease period, the lease will not be renewed at expiration. This policy allows for some late payments, while discouraging a tenant from paying late chronically.

# Establish Expectations for Rent Payment

It is important that tenants know when their rent is due, how it should be paid, and the consequences for not paying on time. One of the covenants in the lease should establish these expectations. It should read something like this:

"Rent payments should be mailed to: (the landlord's address). Rent is due on the first of the month. A late fee of $25 will be assessed when payment is received later than the tenth of the month."

If the lease does not specify that a late charge will be collected and the amount of the charge, such collection cannot be made.

## How the Rent Is to Be Paid

There are several ways in which rent can be collected:

1. The landlord can go to the building on the first of each month and knock on tenants' doors. This is rather inconvenient, and, in some neighborhoods, can be dangerous.

2. The landlord can require that tenants bring the rent in person. Many tenants may resent this requirement, unless there is an office in the building or there is a building manager on site.

3. Tenants can deliver the rent to an on-site manager, who in turn gives the money to the landlord. This is effective, but requires another person to handle the rent payment.

4. The preferred way is to ask tenants to mail the rent to the landlord. This procedure has several advantages:

   A. It places responsibility with the tenant to send the rent, rather than with the landlord to collect the rent.

   B. It avoids the necessity of dealing with cash collections, which can be both dangerous and a potential source of confusion or dispute.

   C. It reduces the amount of time that must be spent with rent collections. To make things easier for the tenants, they can be given pre-addressed envelopes in which to mail the rent payment.

## In What Form Should the Rent Payment Be Made?

Rents should be paid by personal check or money order; avoid accepting second-party checks or cash. Cash collections can be problematic for several reasons:

- *Security:* Handling cash from rent collections increases the risk of theft or robbery.

- *Record keeping:* Checks and money orders should be copied before being deposited, and the copy placed in the tenant's file. Cash payments do not allow for such record keeping.

- *Verification of payment:* If a tenant insists that the rent was paid, a copy of the canceled check or money order is verification. The only verification from a cash payment, however, is a receipt for the money received, which may or may not be accurate.

- *Confusion:* When a tenant hands over 25 or so 20-dollar bills, the possibility of miscounting the money or misplacing one or more of the bills is always present. Many landlords take the position that any payment is better than none at all. If a tenant offers to pay the rent in cash, they reason, it is better to take the money while the tenant has it rather than run the risk that the tenant will not be able to pay later. Such a policy is short-sighted and leads to continued payments by cash or other unacceptable means.

## Collection Letters

When rent is not received on time, tenants should be reminded immediately. On the eleventh of the month, mail a letter to each tenant who has not yet paid the rent, indicating that a late fee has now been assessed (Figure 13–1).

A second collection letter (Figure 13–2) should be mailed on or about the end of the month to each tenant who has still not paid the rent. This letter warns of legal action that will be taken if the rent is not paid within a specified period of time.

## Personal Contact

Some personal contact is appropriate when the rent is late. An on-site manager, for example, should be told who is late with the rent and asked to remind the tenants, but only during chance encounters. The

## Figure 13–1: First Late Rent Letter

July 11, 1992

Herbert Fall
4567 Spring Court Apt. 3B
Chicago IL 60000                    Re: Late Rent

Dear Mr. Fall:

As of the 10th of this month we have not received your rent payment and have now assessed a late payment charge of $25.00.

Your rent is due on the 1st day of each month, and a late payment charge is assessed when your rent remains unpaid as of the 10th day of the month. If there is a problem, please call 555-4488; otherwise, please forward your rent with the $25.00 late charge.

Please mail your check or money order to:

Winters Property Management
1011 Summer Lane
Chicago, IL 60000

Very truly yours,

John Winters

cc: file

## Figure 13–2: Second Late Rent Letter

July 31, 1992

Herbert Fall
4567 Spring Court Apt. 3B
Chicago IL 60000                                   Re: Overdue rent

Dear Mr. Fall:

The month is over and your rent remains unpaid.

Your rent plus a late payment charge of $25.00 must be paid immediately. If payment is not received within 5 days, we will begin legal proceedings for eviction.

Call 555-4488 at once to explain this delinquency, or forward your rent with the $25.00 late charge to:

> Winters Property Management
> 1011 Summer Lane
> Chicago, IL 60000

Very truly yours,

John Winters

cc: file

manager should not be knocking on doors to collect the rent. When a tenant has a history of prompt payments but suddenly is late, it may be helpful to contact the tenant by phone to find out why the rent remains unpaid.

Should a landlord make a personal visit to try to collect the rent? Under most circumstances, such a practice is not advisable. Trying to track down a non-paying tenant is usually difficult and time consuming, because the tenant is not eager to meet with the landlord. If a landlord manages a large number of apartments, there is not time to visit all of the late payers. There are times when visiting a non-paying tenant to collect the rent can even be dangerous. One never knows what mood the tenant might be in when the door is opened. If the tenant is angry already, the sight of a landlord looking for the rent can be just the excuse he or she needs to become violent.

# Chapter

# 14

# When Tenants Do Not Pay the Rent

**M**ost tenants pay their rent promptly. There are also those who are either unable or unwilling to pay on time and need a few reminders. A few tenants, unfortunately, caught without a job or in some other situation—or maybe they are just deadbeats—simply choose to stop paying the rent altogether.

When a tenant has not paid the rent, the response must be based on good business practice and must not be compromised by human emotions. While many cases of non-payment may be rooted in real human tragedy, it is important to remember that managing rental property is a business and a business cannot operate without income. A landlord has an obligation to the other tenants to collect payment for services rendered so that the business can continue to operate and essential services can be provided.

## Excuses

In the course of collecting rents, there will be any number of poignant stories, valid reasons, and reasonable excuses for not paying, such as:

"I just lost my job last week, but I'm sure I will have another job within two weeks, and I'll catch my rent up then."

"My baby got very sick last week, and I had to take him to the emergency room. The doctor's bills have left me a little short this month, but I will catch up next month."

"Since the baby was born, my wife has been unable to work, and this has left us a little short. She will be going back to work in four weeks, and we will catch up on the rent then."

Each of these stories may be true, and each may be a legitimate reason for not having the money to pay the rent. None, however, is a good excuse for not paying the rent. To put the situation into perspective, consider the likely response from the neighborhood grocery store, the gas station, the telephone company, or any other business that offers or provides a necessary service or product. No business can realistically afford to give its products away at no charge, nor can a business operate by extending credit to poor credit risks. Housing is no different from any other necessary business. It is the individual's obligation to locate the money to pay for the product or the individual may not have the product.

Although this attitude may sound cold-hearted, your loyalty and your obligation as the manager of a rental property is to all of the tenants, not just the few who are unable or unwilling to pay the rent. Managing a rental property is not a charity operation; it is a business. And it is amazing how creative some tenants can be in locating money to pay the rent, once the expectation has been established.

## Consistency

Following a precise procedure for rent collection is absolutely essential in a well-managed building. All tenants need to know what to expect from the landlord; all are more comfortable when they understand the expectations and know that everyone will be treated the same. If the landlord shows differential treatment to some tenants, an understandable feeling of resentment and anger is certain to be the result. Additionally, if the landlord does not adhere to his or her own procedures and deadlines, the tenants in the building develop the attitude that the requirements are meaningless. Just like children, many tenants continue to test the landlord's limits until the landlord is finally forced to draw the line.

## Five-Day Notice of Rent Not Paid

When, after receiving the second collection letter, a tenant still has not paid the rent, the next step is to begin an eviction proceeding. In most states, the law requires that a tenant be given a five-day notice of rent due (Figure 14–1) before legal action can be taken. Some communities require that the notice be as long as ten days. Forms for this purpose can be obtained from most office supply or stationery stores, or you can copy Figure 14–1.

A five-day notice may be presented to a tenant as early as the day following the date the rent is due. In practice, however, the five-day notice should be delivered only after other collection efforts have failed.

A five-day notice gives the tenant five days after the serving of the notice to pay the rent in full, making it actually a six-day notice. On the day following the expiration of the five-day period, legal action may be taken. For example, if the five-day notice is delivered on the first of the month, papers may not be filed in court before the seventh.

States are not uniform in their requirements for posting or delivering notices. Check with a local attorney to determine the requirements in your state. In Illinois, the five-day notice must be hand delivered to the tenant, to an occupant who is at least 13 years of age, or to someone who is in charge of the apartment who is at least 13 years of age, such as a baby sitter. Alternatively, the notice may be mailed by registered mail, return receipt requested; but in such a case, the court papers for eviction may not be filed until the receipt has been received.

A five-day notice may not be sent by regular mail or simply slid under the apartment door. It must be served in person or sent registered mail. In the case of a tenant who wants to avoid eviction

## Figure 14–1: Five-Day Notice of Rent Due

# LANDLORD'S FIVE DAYS NOTICE

To: _____. You are hereby notified that there is now due

the owner the sum of $_____, being rent for the premises situated in the City of _____,

County of_____, and State of _____ and known and described as follows, to wit:

_____

together with all buildings, storage areas, recreational facilities, parking spaces and garages used in connection with

said premises.

Rent per month $_____. Rent due from _____ to _____.

And you are further notified that payment of said sum so due has been and is hereby demanded of you, and that unless

payment thereof is made on or before the expiration of five days after service of this notice your lease of said

premises will be terminated _____.

Only FULL PAYMENT of the rent demanded in this notice will waive the landlord's right to terminate the lease

under this notice, unless the landlord agrees in writing to continue the lease in exchange for receiving partial

payment.

_____ is authorized to receive said rent, so due.


Dated this _____ day of _____, 19____


_____

Owner

_____

Agent or Attorney

## AFFIDAVIT OF SERVICE

STATE OF ILLINOIS
COUNTY OF_____

_____, being duly sworn, on oath deposes and says that

on the _____ day of _____, 19____ he served the above notice on the tenant named as follows:

( ) 1. by delivering a copy thereof to the above named tenant, _____.

( ) 2. by delivering a copy thereof to _____, a person above the age of
13 years, residing on or in charge of the above described premises.

( ) 3. by sending a copy thereof to said tenant by certified mail, with request for return of receipt from the
addressee.

( ) 4. by posting a copy thereof on the main door of the above described premises, no one being in actual
possession thereof.


Subscribed and sworn to before me this _____ day

of _____, 19___.

_____

Notary Public

X_____
*Identify the method of service used by placing a check*
*on proper line. Sign on the line marked X.*

proceedings, this requirement can make it difficult for the landlord. Some tenants will refuse to answer the door or accept registered mail. If the apartment appears to be vacated, the notice may be posted on the apartment door (an interior door only, not an exterior door). This is not recommended, however, as the tenant may appear in court and deny receiving the notice, in which case the judge will likely deny the eviction. For the difficult few, a process server can be hired to serve the notice.

If a tenant has promised to pay the rent by a certain day, serve the five-day notice anyway. If the rent is indeed paid, the notice can be torn up. If, however, the rent is not paid as promised, you are in a position to file the necessary papers.

## Filling Out the Five-Day Notice

Before delivering the five-day notice to the tenant, fill out the top part of the form carefully and complete the cover letter (Figure 14–2). Make two copies of the notice, an original and a carbon. Many eviction cases are thrown out of court because of errors in completing the form. Any such error renders the notice invalid and a new notice must then be delivered.

Enter the rent per month on the appropriate line, then the period for which rent is due. If the tenant has paid partial rent for a month, the rent for the entire month is considered due. Rent is not paid until it has been paid in full. In other words, if the monthly rent is $300, and the tenant has paid $150 for June, the amount of rent due is $150, but the period for which the rent is due is June 1 to June 30.

Enter the tenant's name as it appears on the lease on the line following "To:". When filling in the amount due, enter only the actual rent that is due. Do not include late fees, security deposits, or other amounts due. Enter the name of the city in which the apartment is located, along with the name of the county and the state; then enter the complete address of the apartment. If this information is not complete, the sheriff will not pursue the eviction.

Fill in the date that the lease will be terminated. This date must be at least six days after the date on the notice. If the five-day notice is dated the fifth of the month, the termination date must be no earlier than the eleventh. It may, however, be later than that, if desired.

## Figure 14–2: Five-Day Notice Cover Letter

August 6, 1992

Herbert Fall
4567 Spring Court Apt. 3B
Chicago IL 60000

Dear Mr. Fall:

Attached is a 5-day notice, which gives you 5 days within which to pay the entire amount of rent due plus late charges.

If we do not receive such payment before August 12, we will begin legal eviction proceedings.

Please note that vacating the apartment will not relieve you of your obligation to pay the rent for the remaining term of the lease. If you leave without paying, a judgment will be entered against you.

If you have any questions, please call me.

Very truly yours,

John Winters

cc: file

Next, date the notice and sign it. If you are working as an agent for the owner, enter both names.

The bottom of the form may be filled out and notarized any time before the court date. It must be complete and accurate, and signed by the person who actually delivered the notice. This is not necessarily the same name that appears on the notice itself. In some cases you may ask the janitor or the building manager to deliver the notice. If this is the case, their signature must be notarized on the form. Some tenants are eminently familiar with their legal rights, and may challenge the notice in court, so be certain everything is filled out properly.

## When the Notice Has Expired

If the tenant has not paid the rent in full at the conclusion of the five-day notice period, a letter may be sent indicating that legal action is eminent (Figure 14–3). This letter might lead to payment of the rent. If a landlord wishes to be rid of a particular tenant, however, this final letter can be bypassed and legal action begun. The next step is to give the five-day notice, properly filled out, to a qualified attorney who has experience in dealing with legal evictions. It is important to find an experienced attorney for two reasons:

First, time is important in evicting a tenant. An attorney who is unfamiliar with the eviction process may take an excessively long time, which translates into additional loss of rent.

Second, the legal eviction process is not cheap. Legal fees can range from $125 to as high as $350 or $400, sometimes $500. Attorneys who specialize in legal evictions will often handle a case better and for less money than an attorney who handles very few such cases. They can charge lower rates because they handle a large volume of cases.

Court costs for an eviction may range from $75 to $150 and, if it becomes necessary for the sheriff to forcibly evict the tenant, the additional fees can be as much as $200. While not cheap, however, the cost of an eviction should never deter a landlord from proceeding in a timely fashion. If the apartment rents for $500, for example, one month of lost rent equals the entire cost of the eviction proceedings.

## Figure 14–3: Notice of Legal Action

August 13, 1992

Herbert Fall
4567 Spring Court Apt. 3B
Chicago IL 60000

Dear Mr. Fall:

Your past due account has been referred to my attorney. He will file an eviction suit against you within five days. At that time, he will ask for possession of your apartment and for a judgment against you for the outstanding balance in your account plus court costs and attorney's fees. This will appear on your credit report and could result in garnishment of your wages.

If you pay all rents and late charges owed before filing takes place, I will stop the legal action. Thereafter, the only way to remain in your apartment will be to pay all monies owed plus court costs and attorney's fees, which could equal as much as $250.00.

Please note that vacating the apartment will not relieve you of your obligation to pay the rent for the remaining term of the lease. If you leave without paying, a judgment will be entered against you.

Very truly yours,


John Winters

cc: file

## Partial Payment of Rent

Some tenants will offer to pay a portion of the rent due at the expiration of the five-day period. There is no obligation to accept partial payment. If partial payment is accepted, however, the five-day notice must be re-issued, indicating the new amount due.

## The Eviction Process

The actual process of evicting a tenant is both long and time consuming. An eviction does not require the services of an attorney; it can be accomplished by the landlord. Using an attorney, however, is recommended.

The first step is to file eviction papers in the county circuit court and pay the filing fees, at which time a court date is assigned. Typically, this court date will be two or three weeks after the filing. In most cases, the eviction papers will then be served to the tenant by the court.

An appearance in court on the assigned date is mandatory. If the tenant does not appear, the judge typically will order the eviction. If the tenant does appear, the judge may grant a two-week stay to give the tenant time to pay the rent. Some judges will grant up to a month to a tenant who claims to have difficulty finding other housing, or to a tenant with children.

If a stay is granted and the tenant does not pay the rent within the time allowed, another court appearance is necessary, at which time the judge will enter a monetary judgment against the tenant and order the eviction. If the tenant appears and claims hardship, the judge may grant an additional stay.

Once the eviction has been ordered by the judge, the landlord must deliver the eviction order to the county sheriff, who then schedules an eviction date, typically two or three weeks later. At the time the order is delivered, payment is required in an amount to cover the costs involved with the forcible eviction, including the cost of a moving company that will be hired by the sheriff. Typically, this will be around $200, some of which will be refunded if the actual costs are less than that amount. The sheriff will serve these papers to the tenant.

If the tenants have not vacated the apartment by the eviction date, the sheriff brings in a moving company to empty the apartment, the items from the apartment are placed at the curb, and the landlord regains possession of the apartment.

## Avoiding Evictions

The best way to deal with evictions, of course, is to avoid the necessity of an eviction by thoroughly screening new tenants. Unfortunately, no matter how thorough one might be, an occasional problem with non-payment of rent will crop up and an occasional eviction will become necessary.

## Using a Collection Agency

If a tenant leaves owing money because of back rent or excessive damage to the apartment, a collection agency can sometimes be helpful in recovering part of the money owed. Such agencies, which typically work on a contingency basis (their fee is a percentage of the money collected), will need specific information about the former tenant in order to locate them. The best information, of course, is a forwarding address. In lieu of that, a workplace, license plate number, or the emergency phone number from the application can be helpful. Knowing where the former tenant works is useful if wages need to be garnished.

The decision regarding how aggressively to pursue a former tenant for money is often a subjective one. If the person is unemployed and has few resources, sometimes the old saw "you can't get blood from a turnip" comes into play. On the other hand, if the person has the ability to pay and is skipping out on his or her debts, then an aggressive pursuit is probably in order.

# Chapter

# 15

# What to Do When the Lease Is Due to Be Renewed

Retention of good tenants is one of the most important components in operating a successful building. Often, the way in which a lease renewal is handled can mean the difference between keeping a good tenant or losing that tenant to another building. The time to begin thinking about a lease renewal is several months before the lease is due to end.

There are four stages involved in renewing a lease. It is important to follow the procedure carefully, so as to keep pressure on the tenant to make a commitment.

## Stage One: 90 Days before Expiration

Stage one is to mail the initial lease renewal letter (Figure 15–1), accompanied either by a new lease form or a lease renewal rider (Figure

## Figure 15-1: First Lease Renewal Letter

February 1, 1993

Herbert Fall
4567 Spring Court Apt. 3B
Chicago IL 60000

Dear Mr. Fall:

Your current lease will expire on April 30, 1993.

Enclosed are two copies of your renewal lease rider. Please note that your rent increase is $25.00. This increase is unfortunately necessary because of increasing operational expenses, taxes, labor costs and utilities. Because you are a valued tenant, and to encourage you to respond early, I have kept your increase to a minimum. This modest increase, however, is guaranteed only until March 15, after which your rent is subject to an additional $5.00 increase.

Your security deposit will also increase, to reflect the new rental rate. Your new security deposit will be $675.00, an increase of $25.00.

Please sign both copies and return them, along with payment of $25.00 to cover the additional security deposit, to our office no later than March 1 to take advantage of this special incentive. I value your tenancy and hope you plan to stay.

Please sign and return both copies of the renewal rider. One copy will be returned for your records. After March 15, if you decide to renew, I will prepare another renewal rider to reflect the increased amount.

If you have any questions regarding this renewal, please call me at 555-4488.


Very truly yours,


John Winters
Winters Property Management

enc: Lease rider

## Figure 15–2: Lease Renewal Rider

LESSEE:

Herbert Fall
4567 Spring Court Apt. 3B
Chicago IL 60000

This rider becomes a part of and is attached to the lease dated April 22, 1992, by and between John Winters (Lessor) and Herbert Fall (Lessee), covering the premises at 4567 Spring Court, Apt. 3B, Chicago IL 60000, and extends the term of the lease for a period of twelve months from May 1, 1993 to April 30, 1994.

The terms and conditions thereof shall remain in force with the following exceptions, if any:

The rent increases to $675.00 per month.

The new security deposit will be $675.00. This represents an increase of $25.00, which must be received by Lessor to make this rider valid.

Dated this _____ day of _____, 19____

LESSEE:                                        LESSOR:

_____        _____
Herbert Fall                                   John Winters
                                               Winters Property Management

15–2). This first letter should be sent approximately three months before the lease expiration date. If the rent is to be raised, the new lease or the lease renewal rider should indicate the new rent. If the security deposit is to be increased, the amount of the increase should be noted. Any other changes in the conditions of the lease should also be noted.

As an incentive to renew early, the initial letter may offer a special discounted rent increase which will be honored for 30 days following receipt of the letter.

## Stage Two: 60 Days before Expiration

The second lease renewal letter (Figure 15–3), which is sent to all tenants who have not responded to the first letter, should be mailed approximately 60 days before the lease is to end. The purpose of the second letter is to create a sense of urgency: time is growing short and plans must be made to advertise and show any apartments that will become vacant.

Two months is not too early to begin marketing upcoming vacancies. The best prospective tenants often plan their lives far in advance; therefore, a marketing effort should begin as early as possible.

## Stage Three: 45 Days before Expiration

If a tenant does not respond to the second letter, send a third (Figure 15–4) approximately 45 days prior to the end of the lease, informing the tenant that preparations are being made to show the apartment. You should now begin to market the apartments of all tenants who have not replied.

## Figure 15–3: Second Lease Renewal Rider

March 1, 1993

Herbert Fall
4567 Spring Court Apt. 3B
Chicago IL 60000

Dear Mr. Fall:

A reminder that your current lease will expire on April 30, 1993.

I have not yet received your signed lease renewal. I must know soon whether you intend to remain in the apartment, so that I may make preparations to find another tenant.

Please note that your rent increase of $25.00 is guaranteed only until March 15, after which the amount of the renewal will be $30.00.

After March 15, I will begin advertising and showing unrenewed apartments. At that point your renewal will be accepted only if your apartment has not been re-rented to another party.

If you have any questions regarding this renewal, please call me at 555-4488.

Very truly yours,

John Winters
Winters Property Management

## Figure 15–4: Third Lease Renewal Rider

March 15, 1993

Herbert Fall
4567 Spring Court Apt. 3B
Chicago IL 60000

Dear Mr. Fall:

I have not yet received your signed lease renewal. I must know within 24 hours whether you intend to remain in the apartment. Please call immediately to let me know your plans.

If I have heard nothing from you by March 18, I will begin advertising and showing your apartment to prospective tenants. At that point your renewal will be accepted only if your apartment has not been re-rented to another party.

Please call me at 555-4488.

Very truly yours,

John Winters
Winters Property Management

## Figure 15–5: Intention to Vacate

April 1, 1993


Herbert Fall
4567 Spring Court Apt. 3B
Chicago IL 60000

Dear Mr. Fall:

This letter will acknowledge your intention to vacate the above apartment on or before May 1, 1993. Thank you for allowing us to show your apartment to prospective tenants. I realize how disruptive this can be.

On or before the final date of residency we will inspect your apartment. If it is found to be in excellent condition, we will expedite the return of your security deposit of $650.00.

In preparation for that inspection, please check each of the following:

Clean the stove, refrigerator and the kitchen cabinets thoroughly, both inside and outside.

Defrost the refrigerator and leave the dial turned to #1.

Clean bathroom(s) thoroughly. Clean the toilet, the tub, the sink, the vanity inside and out, the medicine cabinet, the floor and the wall tile.

Remove all picture hooks and other items (shelves, etc.) from the walls.

Clean all windows.

Clean out the closets; remove hangers and other items.

Clean light fixtures; replace burned out bulbs.

Be certain that all floors are swept and mopped clean. If there are carpets, have them cleaned.

Clean out your storage locker.

Throw away all packing materials: papers, boxes, string, etc.

Be certain windows are closed and locked.

Repair any damage that is that could be considered beyond normal wear and tear.

Deliver your apartment keys and forwarding address to the janitor or to me.

Thanks for your cooperation in this matter. Please call me at 555-4488 if you have any questions.


Sincerely,


John Winters

## Stage Four: 30 Days before Expiration

The final letter (Figure 15–5) is sent 30 days before the lease is to end, acknowledging that the tenant will be vacating and establishing criteria for refunding the security deposit.

## Establishing a Rent Increase

Increasing the rent can be a ticklish business. The object is to keep pace with increased operating expenses without raising the rent so high as to lose good tenants. Many of the techniques used in Chapter 3 to establish the rent for a vacant apartment should also be used in determining a fair rent increase. In addition, the rate of inflation over the past 12 months should have some impact on rent increases. The local newspaper, which often surveys a number of management firms and apartment owners to determine the size of rent increases during an approaching rental season, can be an additional source of information.

For more information from the professionals, try the local real estate broker's association or the Institute of Real Estate Management of the National Association of Realtors®, P.O. Box 109025, Chicago, Illinois 60610-9025. These organizations can provide general guidelines for rent increases.

The actual amount of the increase will depend entirely on the local situation. If there are vacancies in the building and renting apartments is difficult, the rent increase, if any, should be modest. On the other hand, a strong rental market can dictate greater rent increases. The primary goal, however, is to retain as many good tenants as possible while keeping rents at or near the going rate.

## What If You Choose Not to Renew a Tenant's Lease?

There are any number of reasons not to renew a lease. Perhaps a tenant has often been late with the rent, or has made too much noise,

## Figure 15–6: 30-Day Notice of Non-Renewal

March 27, 1993

Herbert Fall
4567 Spring Court Apt. 3B
Chicago IL 60000

Dear Mr. Fall:

We have decided not to renew your lease, which expires April 30, 1993. On or before the final date of residency we will inspect your apartment. If it is found to be in excellent condition, we will expedite the return of your security deposit of $650.00.

In preparation for that inspection, please check each of the following:

Clean the stove, refrigerator and the kitchen cabinets thoroughly, both inside and outside.

Defrost the refrigerator and leave the dial turned to #1.

Clean bathroom(s) thoroughly. Clean the toilet, the tub, the sink, the vanity, the medicine cabinet, the floor and the wall tile.

Remove all picture hooks and other items (shelves, etc.) from the walls.

Clean all windows.

Clean out the closets; remove hangers and other items.

Clean light fixtures; replace burned out bulbs.

All floors must be swept and mopped clean, and carpets must be professionally cleaned.

Clean out your storage locker.

Throw away all packing materials: papers, boxes, string, etc.

Be certain windows are closed and locked.

Repair any damage that could be considered beyond normal wear and tear.

Deliver your apartment keys and forwarding address to the janitor or to me.

Thanks for your cooperation in this matter. Please call me at 555-4488 if you have any questions.

Sincerely,

John Winters

or has not kept a clean apartment. Whatever the reason, a landlord may choose not to renew a lease, and in most states is under no obligation to tell the tenant the reasons why. Check your local and state laws to determine whether you are obligated to do so. If you are not, it is usually better not to give any reasons in order to avoid possible conflict.

To notify the tenant of your intention not to renew, use a simple letter such as that in Figure 15–6. This letter should be mailed a minimum of 30 days prior to termination of the lease in order to give the tenant adequate time to search for another place to live.

## *Local Laws Vary*

Each state has different laws regarding lease renewals, and local community ordinances vary substantially. It is important to remain current with the applicable laws governing such activity in your state and community.

# Section

# IV

# Working with Employees

The cornerstone of effective property management is service. The people who are most responsible for providing service are the employees who are closest to the tenants: the janitor and the building manager. An enlightened relationship with these key employees will translate into superior service for your tenants and all the dividends that brings: higher retention rates, fewer complaints, lower vacancy rates and lower maintenance costs.

# Chapter

# 16

# Working with a Janitor

**E**ffective property management is built on a foundation of good service; the janitor is one of the persons who provides that service. To be effective, a janitor should exhibit four important characteristics: patience, competence, organization, and a sense of humor.

- *Patience:* A janitor must be patient enough to deal with tenant complaints—and there will be many.

- *Competence:* A janitor must have the skills to complete the various jobs in a professional manner.

- *Organization:* A janitor must be capable of scheduling his or her time in order to complete each job in a timely fashion.

- *Sense of Humor:* It is always helpful if the janitor has a good sense of humor and can develop a good relationship with the tenants.

## What Are the Janitor's Duties?

A janitor has two key responsibilities: to keep the building clean and to complete repairs promptly.

- *A clean building:* The most important part of a janitor's work is to keep the building clean. The building should never look littered, dusty, or dirty. Good tenants expect a clean building.

- *Prompt repairs:* A janitor must respond quickly to tenants' requests, seeing to it that repairs are made in a competent and timely fashion and that no mess is left behind.

## Extra Pay Work

Some janitors, eager to please and taking pride in a good job, will find themselves trying to take care of jobs that should be left to outside contractors. While admirable, such eagerness can focus attention away from the most important part of the janitor's job: to keep the building clean.

Among the jobs that fall within the janitor's purview are fixing leaky faucets, unstopping clogged drains, replacing burned out light bulbs in the common areas, replacing non-working smoke detectors, repairing a broken lock, etc.

If a faucet needs to be replaced, however, an outside contractor should be called in. Likewise, if a drain is worn out and needs to be replaced, if a light fixture needs repair, or if a lock needs to be replaced, they should be done by an outside contractor.

If the janitor is competent and has the time to handle these jobs, they should be done for extra pay. Be careful, however, that the janitor does not shirk his or her primary duties in the quest for extra pay work. Many janitors will offer to redecorate apartments, shampoo carpets, lay floor tile, do interior and exterior painting, and other such jobs for extra pay. If you decide to employ them for these jobs, monitor both the quality of the extra work and whether their routine duties are being completed on time and up to standards.

## The Janitor's Contract

It is often difficult to determine whether a particular job is part of the janitor's routine work. To avoid such misunderstanding, employ a written contract (Figure 16–1). This contract establishes not only the janitor's duties, but also the quality of work that is expected. It also specifies extra pay duties.

Be careful of a contract that establishes only the frequency with which duties are to be performed. A weekly cleaning might not be sufficient to keep some areas of the building clean. When the lobby becomes soiled from tenants tracking in snow and dirt, for example, it should be cleaned immediately rather than waiting for the next scheduled cleaning time.

## How Much Should the Janitor Be Paid?

A janitor's compensation varies greatly from one community to another, making it difficult to establish a guideline. The salary is often based on the number of units in the building. Before agreeing to a compensation package, talk with other property managers and owners to determine the going rate for non-union janitors, and contact the janitor's union to see what union janitors are being paid. This will establish a reasonable salary range for a building of this size. Because the janitor is an important part of your management team, be careful of the penny-wise, pound-foolish syndrome. Paying a high salary, of course, does not guarantee a quality janitor. But be ready to pay a fair salary for a top-notch janitor, and consider adding some incentive bonuses for excellent performance.

## Do You Need a Full-Time or a Part-Time Janitor?

Most buildings of fewer than 50 units, depending on the size of the apartments, do not require a full-time janitor. A common scenario is a part-time janitor who also performs janitorial duties for several other buildings in the area. But each building is different, and the need for

## Figure 16–1: Janitor's Contract

5. Clean all kitchen cabinets.
6. Clean bathroom thoroughly.
7. Aerate and freshen apartment so it smells clean and fresh upon entry.

MISCELLANEOUS:
    A. Deliver letters, 5-day notices and other such communication to tenants when asked.

EXTRA BILLING WORK:
    A. Painting.
    B. Plastering.
    C. Bath tile replacement.
    D. Roof repairs.
    E. Carpet Shampooing.
    F. Materials.

COMPENSATION
    JANITOR will receive a salary of $_____ per month.

This contract will continue in force as long as all duties and obligations are being performed in an acceptable manner. Contract may be ended upon 30 days notice of either party.

Dated this _____ day of _____, 1992

_____
JANITOR

_____
AGENT for MANAGEMENT COMPANY

## Figure 16–1: Janitor's Contract—Page Two

This contract, by and between _____, hereinafter known as MANAGEMENT COMPANY, and _____, hereinafter known as JANITOR, will specify the duties and obligations of JANITOR in respect to the building known as: _____

JANITOR will be expected to perform the following tasks:

CLEANING.
    A. Hallways\staircases will be kept clean and free of litter. Walls will be kept free of smudges and graffiti. Windows on entry doors and vestibule will be kept clean.
    B. Back stairs and area in rear of building will be kept clean and free of litter.
    C. Basement, storage room area and laundry room will be kept free of trash and accumulated tenant cast-offs. Floors will be swept periodically.
    D. Washers and dryers will be kept clean. Laundry room floor will be mopped periodically.
    E. All graffiti will be removed at once.

MAINTENANCE
    A. Replace light bulbs when burned out.
    B. Maintain all smoke detectors in working order. Check at least weekly.
    C. Clean boiler flues at least once a year in the fall.
    D. Repair plumbing leaks and clogged drains as needed.
    E. Repair or replace locks as needed.
    F. Maintain all entry doors and vestibule doors in good secure operating condition.
    G. Replace blinds and shades as needed.
    H. Repair broken windows, screens and hardware on all doors and windows as needed.
    I. Perform carpentry, electrical, plumbing and boiler repairs as needed and when such repairs fall into the category of "routine" or "minor". Arrange for repairs by professional carpenters, plumbers, electricians and boiler repairmen when appropriate.

OPERATIONS
    A. Maintain light timers at an appropriate setting throughout the year.
    B. Maintain boiler timers at an appropriate setting throughout the year.
    C. Oversee operation of all pumps in building and repair or arrange for repairs when needed.
    D. Affix mailbox and doorbell labels when needed.
    E. Perform the following landscaping chores at least weekly during the growing season:
        1. Mow the grass.
        2. Edge the grass.
        3. Trim all hedges and bushes.
        4. Rake all trimmings and leaves and dispose of appropriately.
    F. Keep lawns free of leaves and debris during the fall season.
    G. Seed and fertilize lawns as needed, but at least twice annually.
    H. Remove snow from public walk-ways around the building promptly after each snowfall.
    I. Prepare apartment for tenant move-in when needed, including:
        1. Remove all debris, clutter, etc. from apartment.
        2. Sweep and mop floors, using wax or Mop-N-Glo when appropriate.
        3. Clean carpets, if any.
        4. Clean refrigerator and stove thoroughly.

janitorial services must be assessed individually by taking into account the specific circumstances of the building.

## Should the Janitor Live in the Building?

When a building will not support an on-site manager, a janitor who lives in the building can be an invaluable resource, particularly with a building that is difficult to manage. Every building, no matter how small, should have one on-site person who takes responsibility for overseeing the building. The ideal arrangement is a husband and wife team who live in the building and perform the janitorial duties as well as other tasks, such as showing apartments, delivering notices to tenants, monitoring tenants' behavior in the evenings and on weekends, and reporting any unusual circumstances or events. If a building employs an on-site manager, however, the janitor need not live in the building.

## Should the Janitor Receive a Free Apartment?

In larger buildings, the common practice is to provide a free or reduced rent apartment for an on-site janitor, which becomes part of the janitor's compensation package. A better practice, however, is to pay the entire amount as salary and require the janitor to pay full rent on the apartment. This arrangement makes it very clear how much salary is actually being paid for the job that is being performed.

# Chapter
# 17

# Working with an On-Site Building Manager

**E**very rental property, no matter how small, is easier to manage if someone in the building takes some responsibility for the operation. As the size of the building grows, the need for an on-site manager increases. For many of the simple but time-consuming tasks of management—showing apartments, giving workers access to apartments, monitoring tenant behavior—an effective on-site manager can be invaluable.

For a smaller building, the manager might be a tenant who is paid $50 to $75 per month for very limited responsibilities: to watch over the building and show apartments when they become available. In a larger building, the manager might be a full-time employee who lives in the building and supervises all aspects of the building management.

# Determining Needs

Different buildings have different needs. To determine the need for an on-site manager, consider these factors:

- Size of the building

- Level of difficulty in managing the building

- Location

- Type of apartments

- Type of tenants

- Your personal level of involvement

- Alternative systems for supervising the management of the building

- *Size of the building:* Common sense dictates that the more apartments there are in a building, the more difficult it is to manage. As a rule of thumb, buildings up to 24 units can get by with a part-time janitor/manager who, ideally, would live in the building. The best arrangement is a married couple who share the responsibilities. Above 24 units, it is often better to employ a separate part-time janitor and an on-site manager. These are only rule-of-thumb guidelines, of course; the specific circumstances of your building will dictate the choices you make.

- *Level of difficulty:* A problematic building (Chapter 18) may need a full-time manager, while an easier building of the same size may need only a part-time manager with limited duties.

- *Type of tenant:* A building with a highly transient population will have more need of an on-site manager than one in which the population is relatively stable. Tenants who are potentially more troublesome will need more supervision than tenants who cause few problems.

- *Type of apartments:* Small studio apartments that attract a more transient population of tenants will need greater supervision than a building with larger apartments.

- *Location:* A building located in an unstable area will need more on-site supervision than one located in a more stable neighborhood. Or if the building is located rather far from your home or office, making it more difficult for you to visit the building, an on-site manager can help in the supervision of the building.

- *Your level of involvement:* If you visit the building every day, you may have no need for an on-site manager. If, however, your visits are infrequent, a manager might be essential.

- *Alternative systems:* If you have a brother-in-law who gives the building a great deal of attention, a janitor who responds quickly to all calls for help, or a 24-hour phone line where tenants can receive assistance, an on-site manager might be redundant.

## Characteristics of a Good Building Manager

Managing a rental building is a job that only a few are able to do well. For relatively low pay, the building manager is expected to protect the owner's investment by providing excellent service, fielding complaints, enforcing rules, and keeping apartments rented. To do all of that well, the building manager must have a broad array of skills.

- *Organization:* A good manager is highly organized, able to schedule time efficiently, keep good records, keep a tidy office, and keep appointments.

- *Knows the meaning of clean:* A good manager knows when the building is clean and when it is not. A good manager will see to it that the halls are shining, the windows are sparkling, the doors are smudge-free, and the building is free of trash and debris.

- *People skills:* A good manager knows how to get along with people, how to be firm at the right moments and when to exhibit a sense of humor, when to confront a tenant and when to avoid a confrontation. Aware of the responsibilities of the position, a good manager nevertheless avoids displaying an overbearing attitude.

- *Problem-solver:* A good manager can analyze a problem and seek the right solution. The pressures of managing a property, dealing with tenants, and dealing with repairs and maintenance can combine to overwhelm a person who is not able to take one problem at a time and calmly and efficiently arrive at a solution.

- *Self-confidence:* A good manager exhibits self-confidence without arrogance. This attitude of confidence, in turn, reassures the tenants that the person in charge will take care of their needs.

- *Takes pride in the building:* A good manager considers the building home and takes extra pride in the appearance and the efficient operation of the building.

- *Motivated:* A good manager wants to do a good job, is energetic and goal oriented.

- *Integrity:* A good manager is honest. Because she or he makes decisions every day that affect the success of the business, a good manager must be completely trustworthy.

- *Experienced:* A good manager will have some experience with handling the kinds of problems that will arise in managing a rental property.

## Duties of the On-Site Manager

The job of an on-site manager is geared toward one goal: to keep the building *full of good tenants.* To accomplish that goal, a number of tasks must be done routinely by someone. Some or all of those duties may be assigned to the building manager, depending upon the specific circumstances of the property: the size of the building, whether the manager is full-time or part-time, and how many of the duties you or someone else designated by you will perform. Choose from the following list the duties that will be assigned to your building manager:

1. Rent apartments:

   A. Oversee the preparation of apartments.

   B. Accept phone calls from prospective tenants.

   C. Show apartments to prospective tenants. (A manager who is assigned this duty should be taught the sales skills in Chapter 7.)

   D. Accept applications for apartments

2. Field tenant complaints:
   The manager is the first-line person to receive complaints from tenants. Follow-up should be effective and timely. Three tiers of response are possible:
   *Tier 1:* Take care of the problem.
   *Tier 2:* Assign the problem to the appropriate person.
   *Tier 3:* Notify the property manager (you) or your designated representative.

3. Supervise the building:
   The manager must know what is going on in the building. If a tenant is entertaining too many visitors, if a tenant is causing too much noise, if a tenant has been absent for more than a few days, the manager must be aware and keep the property manager (you) informed.

4. Walk the building every day to make certain the building is safe, clean, and quiet.

5. Supervise the janitor to see that duties are carried out promptly and competently.

6. Miscellaneous duties:

    A. Deliver notices to tenants.

    B. When necessary, appear in court on an eviction proceeding.

    C. If the building does not have individual mailboxes, distribute mail to the tenants.

  7. Report to the property manager (you) on a regular basis.

## The Manager's Contract

Avoid any misunderstanding of duties, goals, or responsibilities by completing a contract with the building manager (Figure 17–1). The contract should specify not only the duties to be performed, but also the level of performance that is expected. This contract will then form the basis for a periodic evaluation conference.

## How to Evaluate the Performance of the Building Manager

Performance evaluation occurs on two levels: informal and formal. The informal evaluation occurs every time you visit the property. While there, tell the manager how well the job is being done: if the building is clean, comment on that; if some of the tenants seem to be noisy, be certain that the manager knows that you noticed. Early in your relationship with a manager, review the goals on a regular basis:

- How many vacancies are there?

- Are any of the tenants causing problems?

- Is the building safe?

- Is the building clean?

- Is the building quiet?

## Figure 17–1: Manager's Contract

This contract, by and between _____, hereinafter known as
MANAGEMENT COMPANY, and _____, hereinafter known
as MANAGER, will specify the duties and obligations of MANAGER in respect to the building
known as: _____

MANAGER will be expected to perform the following tasks:

RENT APARTMENTS
    A. Oversee the preparation of apartments for new tenants. Be certain apartment is clean
and in good repair, carpet is clean, plumbing is in good operating condition, electrical
fixtures work, walls have been painted if necessary, and window shades or blinds are
clean and in good repair.
    B. Receive phone calls from prospective tenants.
    C. Make appointments and show vacant apartments to prospective tenants.
    D. Accept applications for apartments and forward to office for background check.
    E. Conduct move-in inspections with new tenants.
    F. Deliver keys to new tenants and explain how to operate locks, laundry, inter-com, etc.

TENANT SERVICES
    A. Field tenant problems with one of three responses:
        1. Take care of the problem.
        2. Assign the problem to the appropriate person.
        3. Notify the property manager of the problem.
    B. Notify janitor of any problems in or around the building, i.e., burned out light bulbs,
smoke detectors, broken windows, malfunctioning door closers, etc.

SUPERVISE THE BUILDING
    A. Walk the building every day to make certain building is safe, clean and quiet.
    B. Notify janitor and/or property manager of any problems with graffiti, trash, etc.
    C. Notify property manager of any problems with tenants, i.e., noise, visitors, being
absent, etc.

SUPERVISE THE JANITOR
    A. Oversee the janitor to make sure building is clean and tenants receive necessary services
in a timely, courteous and competent manner.
    B. Make sure janitor affixes mailbox and doorbell labels when needed.
    C. Make sure landscaping chores are completed competently and timely during the growing
season.
    D. Be sure janitor removes snow from public walk-ways around the building promptly
after each snowfall.
    E. Supervise the preparation of apartments for tenant move-in, being certain the following
is done well and on time:
        1. All debris, clutter, etc. is removed from apartment.
        2. Floors are swept and mopped, using wax or Mop-N-Glo when appropriate.
        3. Carpets, if any are cleaned.
        4. Refrigerator and stove are cleaned thoroughly.
        5. Kitchen cabinets are cleaned.
        6. Bathroom is cleaned thoroughly.
        7. Apartment is aerated and freshened so it smells clean and fresh upon entry.

## Figure 17–1: Manager's Contract—Page Two

MISCELLANEOUS:
    A. Deliver letters, 5-day notices and other such communication to tenants when asked.
    B. When necessary, appear in court on an eviction proceeding.
    C. Distribute mail to tenants.

COMPENSATION
    MANAGER will receive a salary of $_____ per month.

This contract will continue in force as long as all duties and obligations are being performed in an acceptable manner. Contract may be ended upon 30 days notice of either party.


Dated this _____ day of _____, 1992


_____

MANAGER


_____

AGENT for MANAGEMENT COMPANY

The second level of performance evaluation is based on the contract that you and the manager have signed. Every six months at first, every 12 months thereafter, meet with the manager for a formal evaluation conference. Go over each section of the contract and assess the manager's performance. Ask the manager for his or her perception of their own performance. If your perceptions differ, negotiate a mutually acceptable compromise.

## Compensation Package

A typical compensation package for a building manager will include one or more of the following: salary, incentive pay, free or reduced rent, bonuses. Different managers, because of their different personalities, prefer different types of compensation packages. Work with the manager to tailor a package that will be most agreeable and will result in her or his best performance. Some managers prefer receiving salary only, so they know exactly how much they can count on each month. Others, eager to be compensated for a job well done, prefer a system of incentives and bonuses. Others feel good with reduced rent. Whichever compensation package you choose, the total compensation should be in line with that of other managers in the area. Talk with property management firms, building owners, etc. to determine a reasonable range.

## Establishing Incentives

Many managers work better when they know that hard work will translate into increased pay. For those types of individuals, consider establishing a compensation package that includes performance incentives. The incentives should be tied directly to the manager's goals and should be based on measurable accomplishments.

To be appropriate for an incentive-based compensation package, a goal must be measurable, attainable, and not dependent on the performance of some other person. Keeping the building clean, for example, is not easily measurable. The owner's perception of a clean building may be different from that of the manager. Plus, cleaning the building is typically the responsibility of the janitor, not the manager.

- *Analysis:*

   1. Goal: Keep the building clean.

   2. Is the goal measurable? Not in its present form.

   3. Is the goal attainable? Yes, if you can agree on how to measure it.

   4. Is accomplishment of the goal dependent on someone else's performance? That depends on the job description.

If the manager's contract specifies how the goal of keeping the building clean is to be measured, and also specifies that it is the manager's job to do so, then the goal can be tied to an incentive.

To keep the building full is a measurable goal, and therefore is a likely candidate for an incentive program. Without further refinements, however, the goal flunks the second test, to be attainable.

- *Analysis:*

   1. Goal: Keep the building full.

   2. Is the goal measurable? Yes. The occupancy rate can be measured at any given time.

   3. Is the goal attainable? No. Full occupancy at all times is virtually unattainable. The nature of rental properties is that tenants come and go, even in the best buildings. Therefore, a building might have one or more vacancies because one tenant has left and the apartment has not yet been prepared for a new tenant.

   4. Is accomplishment of the goal dependent on someone else's performance? Yes. But the manager can affect their performance, and probably will if an incentive is involved.

To make the goal more attainable, establish a schedule based on levels of occupancy. For a 50-unit building, the schedule might look like this:

- 0 vacancies in any one month:     $100.00 bonus

- 1 vacancy during the month:       $75.00 bonus

- 2 vacancies:                      $50.00 bonus

If a building is easy to keep full by virtue of its location, amenities, or some other factor, a bonus system based on occupancy rate may not be necessary or appropriate. The beauty of an incentive system is that the property manager can decide where the manager should place his or her primary energies, and then develop an incentive plan that encourages that behavior. Example: One way to keep the occupancy rate high is to keep the renewal rate high. The manager could receive a bonus each time a tenant renews a lease, or an annual bonus based upon a percentage of the number of tenants who renewed.

Example of a lease renewal incentive system:

- For each lease renewal, the building manager will receive $75. Alternatively, the manager will receive an annual bonus based on the percentage of tenants who renew their leases for a full 12 months:

  1. 100 percent renewals:     $500 bonus

  2. 90 percent renewals:      $400 bonus

  3. 80 percent renewals:      $300 bonus

- *Analysis:*

  1. Goal: At least 80 percent of the present tenants will renew their leases when they expire.

  2. Is the goal measurable? Yes.

  3. Is the goal attainable? Yes.

  4. Is accomplishment of the goal dependent on someone else's performance? Yes. Both the janitor and the property manager have some impact on whether good tenants renew their leases. But the manager can significantly affect how those individuals perform their work.

A manager's goal is not only to keep the building full, however. The second part of the goal is to keep the building full with *good tenants*. While the occupancy rate and the renewal rate are easily measured, the quality of the tenants is not. Therefore, an incentive based upon full or nearly full occupancy is reasonable, while an incentive based upon a vague notion like "good tenants" is not.

- *Analysis:*

  1. Goal: To keep good tenants in the building.

  2. Is the goal measurable? No.

  3. Is the goal attainable? Yes, if it could be measured.

  4. Is accomplishment of the goal dependent on someone else's performance? Partially. Both the janitor and the property manager have some impact on whether good tenants stay in the building, but the building manager can significantly affect how those individuals perform their work.

Avoid any incentive that is based on vague, non-measurable criteria. When it comes time to determine whether a bonus should be granted, you and the manager will be unable to agree on the accomplishment of the goal. Such disagreement can lead to resentment and anger.

Avoid also any incentive that encourages the wrong behavior. For example, avoid paying an incentive for renting apartments (example: $25 each time an apartment is rented). Such an incentive encourages a high turnover rate and poor selectivity of tenants and discourages long-term tenants and low turnover.

# Section

# V

# Special Circumstances

**M**any buildings are rather forgiving; they can survive for years with mediocre management. Survive, but not thrive. A problem building, on the other hand, may offer only one choice: manage it well or lose it. The key: maintain a safe, clean, quiet building.

# Chapter

# 18

# How to Apply Your Management Skills to a Problem Building

**W**hile no rental property is truly easy to manage—all require dedication and hard work—some buildings are more problematic than others. The problems presented by such buildings are not necessarily different from those encountered with other rental properties, but they are more intense and potentially more explosive.

A problem building is one that either exhibits or has the potential to exhibit higher than average vacancy rates, greater than normal repair and maintenance costs, extensive rent collection problems, and a relatively high eviction rate. In a problem building, the property manager must be constantly vigilant to screen out less desirable tenants, and top-quality tenants are more difficult to attract. Just keeping a problem building clean can be a major task, and repairs are a constant fact of life. Collecting the rent is often a struggle.

Most management firms and the majority of property owners steer clear of problem buildings, assuming that the reward is not worth the hassle. The fact is, however, that problem buildings can be profitable if they are handled correctly. Even under seemingly impossible circumstances, such buildings can be managed successfully.

## Factors That Produce a Problem Building

A number of factors can work to make a building problematic. The most obvious ingredient would seem to be the quality of the neighborhood, but that would be a misperception. Often the neighborhood is a minor contributing factor. The specific location of the building, however, regardless of the surrounding neighborhood, is a major element in a problem building. The types of apartments also play a major role, as does a lack of amenities. A bad reputation can be particularly difficult to overcome, and recovering from prior mismanagement requires a careful strategy. Transient tenants create a unique set of management problems. Alone or together, each of these factors can create a problem building, one that requires special attention and careful handling.

### Location

Common sense dictates that the best prospective tenants, with a wide variety of choices available to them, typically choose the most favored places to live. As a result, a building that is situated in an undesirable location will tend to attract a less desirable group of tenants.

The most obvious is a building located in a high crime-rate area. With all of the issues associated with such an environment—crumbling infrastructure, vacant buildings, vacant lots, unemployment—management problems can be intense. High-crime neighborhoods do not hold a monopoly on management problems, however. In low-crime areas, location can still create difficulties. A building located too close to a railroad track or on a busy street, for example, will discourage a considerable number of prospective tenants. Many people prefer not to live across from a school, next to a busy parking lot, or in a densely populated neighborhood. Each of these locations presents unique management problems.

## High Turnover

A building with a high tenant turnover rate is more problematic to manage than one with a stable population.

## Small Apartments

Regardless of location, a building with a majority of single-room or small studio apartments will attract a more transient population than one that offers larger apartments. Tenants tend to grow out of a small apartment, gathering treasures that require one or two bedrooms.

## Lack of Amenities

A building that offers modernized kitchens and bathrooms tends to attract better tenants than an 80-year-old building with a wall-hung kitchen sink and a few pantry shelves. Amenities alone, however, are no guarantee of a good population of tenants.

## Reputation

A beautiful building, offering the best amenities, in a good location, may have developed a reputation for housing prostitutes, drug dealers, or other such elements. Legitimate or not, such a reputation will discourage better tenants from living there.

## Prior Mismanagement

A building that has been mismanaged will continue to present management problems for some time to come. Less than one year of mismanagement may have driven the majority of the good tenants away. They in turn will have been replaced by less desirable tenants who will be difficult to remove. As long as the bad tenants remain, however, good tenants will be difficult to attract.

# How to Manage a Problem Building

To manage a problem building, use the same procedures that are employed in the operation of any other building, but apply those procedures with greater intensity and consistency. A troublesome building leaves a much smaller margin for error, and the consequences for dilly-dallying can be extreme. There is one certainty with a difficult-to-manage building: to be successful you will need to invest more of your time than with other properties.

## *Assess Specific Needs*

There are three basic requirements for any well-managed property: the building must be clean, safe, and quiet. The first step is to assess the building on the basis of these criteria. If the building is not clean, safe, and quiet, move quickly to rectify the situation.

### Clean

The front of the building must look clean and inviting. If any of the common areas are dirty, clean them, paint them, fix them. Repair tattered screens, sagging doors, broken locks. Replace worn and tattered carpeting, broken tile, and worn out linoleum. In other words, make the building look clean and inviting.

### Safe

Maintaining building security is a two-fold effort. First, tenants must feel safe from outside threats. Exterior doors must close and lock securely, intercom systems must work flawlessly, security bars must be secure. Discourage loitering around the building by posting notices and sending letters to the tenants.

Second, tenants must feel safe from their fellow tenants. Rid the building as quickly as possible of loiterers and unsavory types. Evict tenants who have a lot of traffic through their apartments. Tenants who entertain a large number of friends on a regular basis must be asked to leave.

When ridding a building of unsavory or potentially dangerous tenants, however, be careful to follow established legal procedures.

If tenants are on a month-to-month basis, the simplest way to get rid of an undesirable tenant is through non-renewal, which requires no statement of cause. A 30-day notice of termination (Figure 18–1) is sufficient. This notice must be delivered to the tenant prior to the first day of the final month of tenancy. If the tenant refuses to surrender possession on the last day of the month, legal action should be taken.

If a tenant has a 12-month lease, other alternatives must be used. Look for actions that are in violation of specific provisions of the lease (e.g., loud noise, too many occupants in the apartment, etc.). Use a ten-day notice of termination (Figure 18–2) and follow up with eviction proceedings. Be prepared, however, for a judge who may side with the tenant and block the eviction. If the tenant is slow to pay the rent, use a five-day notice and follow the eviction procedures outlined in Chapter 14. There is no need to wait until the tenant is seriously overdue before taking action, but be careful that your actions are consistent with other late payers. Whichever procedure you choose to follow, be careful not to violate the provisions of any applicable state or local laws, and engage the services of an attorney who has experience with eviction proceedings.

### Quiet

Walk the building at various times, listening for excessive noise. If tenants are creating more noise than is acceptable—through loud music, loud TV, noisy children, noisy arguments, etc.—serve them with a warning letter. If the noise continues, deliver a notice of termination (ten-day notice) and proceed with an eviction.

## Establish Expectations

In a troublesome building, tenants must know the rules. These rules must be fair, clearly stated, and consistently enforced. Communicate the rules through a lease rider (Chapter 10, Figure 10–3). If tenants do not presently have leases, draft a new lease for each tenant that includes the rules for the building. If tenants have leases, circulate a list of the building rules to each of the present tenants, and include the rules as a rider on all new leases and lease renewals.

## Figure 18-1: 30-Day Notice of Termination

To: _____. You are hereby notified that your month to

month tenancy or lease of the premises situated in the city of _____,

County of _____, and State of Illinois and known and described as follows, to wit:

_____

together with all buildings, storage areas, recreational facilities, parking spaces and garages used in connection with

said premises, will be terminated as follows:

The undersigned elects to terminate your month to month tenancy of said premises, such termination will be

effective on the _____ day of _____, 19____, and you are hereby notified to quit and

deliver up possession at that time.

Dated this _____ day of _____, 19____

_____

Owner

_____

Agent or Attorney

### AFFIDAVIT OF SERVICE

STATE OF ILLINOIS
COUNTY OF_____

_____, being duly sworn, on oath deposes and says that

on the _____ day of _____, 19____ he served the above notice on the tenant named as follows:

(  ) 1. by delivering a copy thereof to the above named tenant, _____.

(  ) 2. by delivering a copy thereof to _____, a person above the age of
13 years, residing on or in charge of the above described premises.

(  ) 3. by sending a copy thereof to said tenant by certified mail, with request for return of receipt from the
addressee.

(  ) 4. by posting a copy thereof on the main door of the above described premises, no one being in actual
possession thereof.

Subscribed and sworn to before me this _____ day

of _____, 19___.

_____

Notary Public

X_____

*Identify the method of service used by placing a check
on proper line. Sign on the line marked X.*

## Figure 18–2: 10-Day Notice of Termination for Cause

To: _____. You are hereby notified that your tenancy or

lease of the premises situated in the city of _____, County of _____, and

State of Illinois and known and described as follows, to wit: _____

_____

together with all buildings, storage areas, recreational facilities, parking spaces and garages used in connection with said premises, will be terminated. You have breached or are in default of the terms of your lease for said premises, as follows: _____

_____

The owner has elected to terminate your right of possession under the lease, and you are hereby notified to quit and deliver up possession of the same to the owner within ten (10) days after service of this notice.

Dated this _____ day of _____, 19____

_____
                                                                    Owner

_____
                                                        Agent or Attorney

### AFFIDAVIT OF SERVICE

STATE OF ILLINOIS
COUNTY OF_____

_____, being duly sworn, on oath deposes and says that

on the _____ day of _____, 19____ he served the above notice on the tenant named as follows:

( )  1. by delivering a copy thereof to the above named tenant, _____.

( )  2. by delivering a copy thereof to _____, a person above the age of
13 years, residing on or in charge of the above described premises.

( )  3. by sending a copy thereof to said tenant by certified mail, with request for return of receipt from the
addressee.

( )  4. by posting a copy thereof on the main door of the above described premises, no one being in actual
possession thereof.

Subscribed and sworn to before me this _____ day
of _____, 19___.

_____
Notary Public

X_____
*Identify the method of service used by placing a check
on proper line.  Sign on the line marked X.*

### *Enforce the Rules*

Once the rules are in place, their only value lies in firm and consistent enforcement. Use warning letters when appropriate and eviction proceedings when necessary. Remember that your primary obligation is to serve the needs of the majority of the tenants who do not cause problems, not the few who do. Do not allow tenants to slide by out of concern for their well-being.

### *Be Consistent*

Because of the volatile nature of this kind of building, the response to any problem, no matter how small, must be quick and consistent. Responses to noisy tenants and tenants who cause problems must be swift and fair. Letters of reminder, notices and eviction proceedings must occur consistently and on schedule. It is far too easy to establish a climate in which tenants expect to slide by. Establish the expectation that rents will be paid on time and rules will be followed or tenants will leave. Good tenants must know that their rights to a safe, clean, and quiet home are being protected by the property manager.

### *Screen Tenants Carefully*

Many of the individuals who apply for an apartment in a problem building will be undesirable. Therefore, prospective tenants must be carefully and thoroughly screened. Follow the procedures in Chapter 9, but be even more vigilant. A mistake in screening can have disastrous results in this kind of building. One bad tenant can quickly drive out several good ones.

### *Train and Supervise Your Employees*

In a building that is difficult to manage, employees must be taught to recognize and deal effectively with potentially serious problems. Because they are the front-line people, they must know the importance of maintaining a clean, quiet, and safe building. They must be firm without being belligerent. They must be confident without being arrogant. They must enforce the rules without being confrontational. And they must report any indications of wrongdoing on the part of the tenants.

# Section

# VI

# Taking Care of Business

**P**roperty management is a business that involves all the standard operations required of any business venture. Two of the most important tasks—but also the most easily procrastinated—are accounting and property maintenance. Either can be handled personally or delegated to professionals. Either way, however, each must be given the attention it requires; neither can be long ignored.

# Chapter

# 19

## How to Handle the Accounting

The most easily overlooked part of building management is the bookkeeping. After dealing with leases, contractors, janitors, tenant problems and all the other management activities that consume your time and energy, the accounting is easy to ignore. It doesn't even sound like fun! At the end of the year, however, when it comes time to file a tax return, you may find it difficult to sort through a bushel basket of invoices, an incomplete checkbook, and a mass of rent receipts. Better to allocate a specific time each month to catch up on all the bookkeeping.

## By Hand, with a Computer, or by a Professional?

Some owners/managers prefer to keep the books the old-fashioned way: manually in a ledger book. With only a few rental units, manual bookkeeping can be done very easily.

Alternatively, managers who are not afraid to tackle a computer (My normal inclination is to tackle the computer, literally, and kick it through the goal posts. But not everyone finds computers to be as impertinent as I do.) will find a wide selection of predesigned property management software on the market. Relatively simple to use, computer software offers a number of advantages over manual bookkeeping: time savings (if you can figure out what to do), accuracy and a broad array of functions.

The third alternative is to use a professional bookkeeping service. Each month the records are delivered to the accountant's office and, a few days later, a complete set of accounting records are returned. While simple, this system can be expensive.

## Developing an Accounting System

Either manually or with a basic computer, you can develop a simple accounting system. An effective system includes three basic parts:

- The rent schedule, which includes all income from the property

- The cash disbursements journal

- An operating statement or cash flow statement

The forms used in this chapter are designed to be used with accountant's ledger sheets. If you decide to use a computer, the forms translate well onto a spread sheet program. Keep in mind that this is a simple system. If you need to keep track of more data than these forms allow for, or if you need greater sophistication for any reason, ask an accountant with some experience with rental properties to help design a system. Alternatively, several of the property management software systems listed in the Appendix offer accounting packages that may better suit your needs. Everything you find, however, will likely be a variation of the three forms that follow.

# Figure 19–1: Rent Schedule

Building _____

Year _____

| Unit | Name | Sec Dep | Rent | Jan | Feb | Mar | April | May | June | July | Aug | Sept | Oct | Nov | Dec | Total |
|---|---|---|---|---|---|---|---|---|---|---|---|---|---|---|---|---|
| Store | Hakimi | $2,500 | $1,500 | $1,500 | $1,500 | | | | | | | | | | | |
| Store | Zidek | 2,750 | 1,750 | 1,750 | 1,750 | | | | | | | | | | | |
| Apt 2A | McNeilly | 625 | 625 | 625 | 625 | | | | | | | | | | | |
| Apt 3A | Berg | 615 | 615 | 615 | 615 | | | | | | | | | | | |
| Apt 4A | McCoy | 1,250 | 625 | 0 | 625 | | | | | | | | | | | |
| Apt 2B | Ro | 935 | 620 | 1240 | 0 | | | | | | | | | | | |
| Apt 3B | O'Toole | 635 | 635 | 635 | 635 | | | | | | | | | | | |
| Apt 4B | Hagen | 650 | 650 | 650 | 650 | | | | | | | | | | | |
| Apt 2C | Van Tassel | 615 | 615 | 615 | 615 | | | | | | | | | | | |
| Apt 3C | Pruchno | 615 | 615 | 615 | 615 | | | | | | | | | | | |
| Apt 4C | Vierthaler | 635 | 635 | 635 | 635 | | | | | | | | | | | |
| Gar #1 | McNeilly | 65 | 65 | 65 | 65 | | | | | | | | | | | |
| Gar #2 | Hagen | 65 | 65 | 65 | 65 | | | | | | | | | | | |
| Gar #3 | Pruchno | 105 | 70 | 70 | 70 | | | | | | | | | | | |
| Total rent | | | $9,085 | $9,080 | $8,465 | | | | | | | | | | | |
| Laundry Income | | | | 127 | 89 | | | | | | | | | | | |
| Miscellaneous | | | | 316 | 75 | | | | | | | | | | | |
| Total Income | | | | $9,523 | $8,629 | | | | | | | | | | | |

## *Rent Schedule*

A simple rent schedule (Figure 19–1) lists each source of rental income, which includes apartment rent, commercial rent, garage rent, parking space rent and storage space rent, along with other income. For each rental unit, list the unit number or other designation, the tenant's name, the amount of security deposit paid and the scheduled rent. When a tenant pays the rent, enter the amount under the appropriate month. If you keep up with the record keeping, a glance at the rent schedule will reveal which tenants are behind with their rent.

Some owners like to keep a separate record of when the rents are paid (Figure 19–2), then transfer the information to the Rent Schedule and the Cash Flow Statement when they do the books at the end of the month. This monthly form allows you to enter the date when the rent is paid, the amount paid, the date the rent is paid through, and any balance that may be due. A glance at the form reveals which rents are yet to be paid.

- *Laundry:* All money taken from the laundry machines is registered as income to the property.

- *Miscellaneous:* Miscellaneous income includes money received for application fees, late charges, credit check fees, return check charges, storage fees, etc. Keep a separate itemized list of all miscellaneous income in a receipts ledger (Figure 19–3).

- *Security Deposits:* Security deposits constitute a cash receipt but are not considered income, since all such deposits will have to be returned at some time. Some owners keep security deposits in a separate account and maintain a separate listing of who has paid and the amount. In some circumstances, usually involving larger buildings, interest must be paid on security deposits. Check your local and state ordinances to determine whether you must pay interest. If so, you might want to keep all security deposits in an interest-bearing account.

  A security deposit is transformed into income when it is used to cover unpaid rent or to pay for repairs to a vacated apartment. When you withhold part or all of a security deposit to cover cleaning expenses or repairs the amount must be en-

## Figure 19–2: Rent Payment Records

Building _____     Month __January__, 19 _92_

| RECEIVED FROM | APT | DATE | AMOUNT | PAID FROM | PAID TO | BAL DUE |
|---|---|---|---|---|---|---|
| Hakimi | Store | 12/29 | 1,500 | 1/1/92 | 1/31/92 | -0- |
| Zidek | Store | 12/28 | 1,750 | 1/1/92 | 1/31/92 | -0- |
| McNeilly | 2A | 1/7 | 625 | 1/1/92 | 1/31/92 | -0- |
| Berg | 3A | 1/2 | 615 | 1/1/92 | 1/31/92 | -0- |
| McCoy | 4A | | | | | 625 |
| Ro | 2B | 12/28 | 1,240 | 1\1\92 | 2\28\92 | -0- |
| O'Toole | 3B | 12/29 | 635 | 1/1/92 | 1/31/92 | -0- |
| Hagen | 4B | 1/21 | 650 | 1/1/92 | 1/31/92 | -0- |
| Van Tassel | 2C | 1/3 | 615 | 1/1/92 | 1/31/92 | -0- |
| Pruchno | 3C | 1/18 | 615 | 1/1/92 | 1/31/92 | -0- |
| Vierthaler | 4C | 12/25 | 635 | 1/1/92 | 1/31/92 | -0- |
| McNeilly 2A | Gar #1 | 1/7 | 65 | 1/1/92 | 1/31/92 | -0- |
| Hagen 4B | Gar #2 | 1/21 | 65 | 1/1/92 | 1/31/92 | -0- |
| Pruchno 3C | Gar #3 | 1/18 | 70 | 1/1/92 | 1/31/92 | -0- |

## Figure 19–3: Miscellaneous Receipts Ledger

Building _____     Year _____

| DATE | RECEIVED FROM | PURPOSE | AMOUNT | TOTAL |
|---|---|---|---|---|
| 1/5 | Hagen 4B | Late charge | 25.00 | |
| 1/7 | Paul Stone | App fee | 25.00 | |
| 1/7 | George Jones | App fee | 25.00 | |
| 1/18 | Pruchno 3C | Late charge | 25.00 | |
| 1/21 | Sally Struthers 2B | Relet fee | 200.00 | |
| 1/24 | McCoy 4A | Storage fee | 15.00 | |
| | | | | 315.00 |
| 2/15 | Hagen 4B | Late charge | 25.00 | |
| 2/17 | Amelia Turner | App fee | 25.00 | |
| 2/19 | Joe Fisher | App fee | 25.00 | |
| | | | | 75.00 |

tered as miscellaneous income. When you use a security deposit to cover unpaid rent, enter the amount as rental income under the appropriate rental unit.

## *Disbursements Journal*

During the month, as you pay the bills, keep accurate information in the check register. Some owners like to make photocopies of each check before it is sent, to be sure no mistakes are made. Alternatively, try using a checkbook that produces an NCR copy of each check that is written. At the end of the month, when the bills have been paid, take time to enter each payment in the Disbursements Journal (Figure 19–4). Include the check number and the name of the payee, and enter the correct amount under the appropriate heading. Column headings in the Disbursements Journal should correspond with the line items in the Cash Flow Statement (Figure 19–5).

### Line Items

Most line items are self-explanatory. A few need additional explanation:

- *Mortgage:* The mortgage payment may include principal, interest, and an escrow payment to cover future taxes and insurance premiums. The portion of the mortgage payment that is applied to the principal—the part that actually pays back the loan—is not considered an expense for tax purposes. Interest, taxes and insurance are. Therefore, you must devise some simple way to note how the mortgage payment breaks down into each of these four items.

  If you pay the insurance and taxes yourself (if there is no escrow account), the mortgage payment will include only principal and interest. If you know how much is interest and how much is principal (your lender can provide an amortization schedule), enter those two figures in the Cash Flow Statement as in Figure 19–5. If you prefer not to be bothered, then enter the entire mortgage payment as one disbursement and divide it up later.

  The simplest way to deal with the mortgage payment is to

# Figure 19-4: Disbursements Journal

Building _____ Month __January__ 19 ___

| Paid To | Ck # | Mortgage | Taxes | Insurance | Gas | Electric | Water | Repairs | Maint | Supplies | Scavenger | Advertising | Legal |
|---|---|---|---|---|---|---|---|---|---|---|---|---|---|
| Gas Company | 234 | | | | 2,345 | | | | | | | | |
| Welding Service | 235 | | | | | | | 445 | | | | | |
| Water Company | 236 | | | | | | 368 | | | | | | |
| Pest Control | 237 | | | | | | | | 60 | | | | |
| Electric Company | 238 | | | | | 216 | | | | | | | |
| Corner Hardware | 239 | | | | | | | | | 123 | | | |
| Trash Hauler | 240 | | | | | | | | | | 150 | | |
| Corner Hardware | cash | | | | | | | | | 35 | | | |
| Painter | 241 | | | | | | | 231 | | | | | |
| Janitor | 242 | | | | | | | | 450 | | | | |
| Mortgage Company | 243 | 3,600 | | | | | | | | | | | |
| | | 3,600 | | | 2,345 | 216 | 368 | 676 | 510 | 158 | 150 | | — |

Building _____ Month __February__ 19 ___

| Paid To | Ck # | Mortgage | Taxes | Insurance | Gas | Electric | Water | Repairs | Maint | Supplies | Scavenger | Advertising | Legal |
|---|---|---|---|---|---|---|---|---|---|---|---|---|---|
| Electric Company | 244 | | | | | 254 | | | | | | | |
| Roofing Company | 245 | | | | | | | 1,533 | | | | | |
| Water Company | 246 | | | | | | 423 | | | | | | |
| Pest Control | 247 | | | | | | | | 60 | | | | |
| Gas Company | 248 | | | | 2,819 | | | | | | | | |
| Mortgage Company | 249 | 3,600 | | | | | | | | | | | |
| Trash Hauler | 250 | | | | | | | | | | 150 | | |
| Insurance Company | 251 | | | 435 | | | | | | | | | |
| Janitor | 252 | | | | | | | | 450 | | | | |
| Corner Hardware | 253 | | | | | | | | | 237 | | | |
| | | 3,600 | | 435 | 2,819 | 254 | 423 | 1,533 | 510 | 237 | 150 | | — |

# Figure 19–5: Cash Flow Statement

Building _____                    Year _____

| | BUDGETED | | ACTUAL | | | | | | | | | | | | |
| | annual | monthly | Jan | Feb | Mar | April | May | June | July | Aug | Sept | Oct | Nov | Dec | Total |
|---|---|---|---|---|---|---|---|---|---|---|---|---|---|---|---|
| **RECEIPTS** | | | | | | | | | | | | | | | |
| Rent | 103,569 | 8,630 | 9,080 | 8,465 | | | | | | | | | | | |
| Laundry | 1,200 | 100 | 127 | 89 | | | | | | | | | | | |
| Misc | 1,200 | 100 | 315 | 75 | | | | | | | | | | | |
| Total Receipts | 105,969 | 8,830 | 9,522 | 8,629 | | | | | | | | | | | |
| **DISBURSEMENTS** | | | | | | | | | | | | | | | |
| Mortgage | 43,200 | 3,600 | | | | | | | | | | | | | |
| Principal | | | 276 | 280 | | | | | | | | | | | |
| Interest | | | 3,324 | 3,320 | | | | | | | | | | | |
| Real Estate Taxes | 5,200 | 433 | | | | | | | | | | | | | |
| Insurance | 1,600 | 133 | | 435 | | | | | | | | | | | |
| Utilities | | | | | | | | | | | | | | | |
| Gas | 18,500 | 1,542 | 2,345 | 2,819 | | | | | | | | | | | |
| Electric | 2,400 | 200 | 216 | 254 | | | | | | | | | | | |
| Water | 4,800 | 400 | 368 | 423 | | | | | | | | | | | |
| Repairs & Decorating | 15,000 | 1,250 | 676 | 1,533 | | | | | | | | | | | |
| Maint & Cleaning | 5,400 | 450 | 510 | 510 | | | | | | | | | | | |
| Supplies | 3,600 | 300 | 158 | 237 | | | | | | | | | | | |
| Scavenger | 1,800 | 150 | 150 | 150 | | | | | | | | | | | |
| Advertising | 1,200 | 100 | | | | | | | | | | | | | |
| Legal | 1,000 | 83 | | | | | | | | | | | | | |
| Total Disbursements | 103,700 | 8,641 | 8,023 | 9,961 | | | | | | | | | | | |
| Net Cash Flow | 2,269 | 189 | 1,499 | -1,332 | | | | | | | | | | | |

carry it as one expense item month by month and divide it up for tax purposes at the end of the year. Your lender will probably send you a statement early in January indicating how much interest was paid during the preceding year, how much was applied to the principal of the loan and, if you have an escrow account, how much was paid for taxes and insurance. Wait until you receive that statement to divide the mortgage payment among its respective categories.

In the meantime, each month when you write the check for your mortgage payment enter the total amount of the check in the Disbursements Journal (Figure 19-4) and carry it over to the Cash Flow Statement (Figure 19-5) as an expense item, even though part of the payment—the amount that goes into the escrow account—is not legitimately an expense. Think of the escrow account as a separate checking account, although one from which someone else will write the checks. In other words, the escrow payment is cash that has been transferred from one available source—your checkbook—to another available source—the mortgage company's checkbook.

- *Repairs:* Repairs include actual cost—parts and labor—for repairs to plumbing, electrical, heating and air-conditioning, appliances, broken windows, broken door locks, etc. Typically, such expenses involve outside contractors who submit a bill for labor and materials. Sometimes the work may be done by the janitor as an extra-pay duty. For do-it-yourself work, assign only the cost of the materials.

- *Maintenance and cleaning:* Include labor costs only. Supplies appear in a separate line item.

## Cash Flow Statement

The Cash Flow Statement (Figure 19-5) ties the income and the expenditures together and produces a monthly profit/loss statement. At the top of the form, carry over all income totals from the Rent Schedule (Figure 19-1). Under Disbursements, enter the total from each column in the Disbursements Journal on the corresponding line in the Cash Flow Statement. Add up the disbursements, subtract from the receipts total, and you have the monthly cash flow, either positive or negative.

### Physical Receipts

Keep all physical receipts for labor and materials in a safe, dry place. A tax audit, should one occur, will likely be requested as much as two or three years after the end of the present tax year. An inability to produce receipts to document expenses will result in significantly higher taxes. Before filing the receipts away, take the time to organize them by line item title and by month. Should you be audited, this will significantly reduce the amount of time necessary to prepare for the audit.

## Should You Have More Than One Checking Account?

If you manage only one building, a single checking account works nicely. With more than one property, however, you must decide whether to maintain one checkbook or to open a separate account for each property. There are good reasons for going either way.

- *Opening a separate account for each building simplifies accounting procedures:* the checkbook functions as a crude balance sheet. Although the practice is not recommended, if one is less than conscientious about keeping up with the accounting a separate checkbook helps keep the figures straight.

    For the manager who is conscientious about keeping up with the accounting, however, a single checkbook is a better alternative. Keeping records on several properties while writing checks from one checkbook is a relatively simple and easy process, particularly if you use a computer. If you choose to use one checkbook, however, be certain to make full and complete notes on each check and on each entry in your checkbook register. Indicate the name of the property, which apartment, and for what purpose the check was written.

- *Adding Personal Funds:* If the checking account is short one month because expenses have exceeded income, you will need to deposit personal funds into the account. When you do so, note the source of the funds in the check register and make a copy of the check. In your records keep all personal money separate from rental income. Do not enter such payments in the Rent Schedule or the Cash Flow Statement.

- *Copy all checks, deposit slips and money orders:* The less you trust to memory the better. Before making any deposits to the checking account, photocopy all items for your records. If a check or money order does not indicate the purpose for which it was received, write it on the face of the check before making the copy.

## Use the Accounting System to Help Manage Your Property

Successful property management requires maintaining a balance between income and expenses. If expenses exceed income, it becomes necessary either to inject new capital into the venture, to reduce expenditures or to increase income—perhaps all three. If rents have been established at fair market levels and cannot be raised (Chapter 3) and you are reluctant to infuse new capital into the venture, the only answer is to reduce expenditures. Accurate and timely accounting will reveal which expenses, if any, can be reduced and by how much.

### Managing by Budget

The sample Cash Flow Statement (Figure 19–5) includes a budgeted amount (both annual and monthly) for each line item. These figures provide a benchmark for operating the property. A realistic budget should be based upon the property's past performance. If you are new to a property, develop a budget based upon experience with similar properties. If your experience with rental properties is limited, follow the guidelines in my book *Making Real Money in Rental Properties,* by the same publisher, to establish a realistic budget. Aimed at the would-be investor, that book explains how to project with some degree of accuracy the actual income and expenses for various types of rental properties.

The goal in managing a property by budget is to maintain income at or above the projected budget levels while holding expenses within the projected parameters. To establish a realistic income projection, first refer to the Rent Schedule (Figure 19–1) to determine the gross scheduled income for the property. Then reduce that by a figure that represents projected rates of vacancy and non-collection. In the example, the scheduled income was reduced by 5 percent. With a more difficult building, that figure should likely be 10 percent or even 15 percent. Use your best judgment to arrive at a figure that is most realistic.

Expense projections should combine the historical performance of the property itself with known performance of similar properties. Fixed expenses like mortgage payments and utility costs can be estimated with some degree of accuracy. The true cost of repairs and maintenance, however, is always elusive and difficult to pin down. As a rule of thumb, the cost of repairs is always substantially higher than one would expect. In the example, $15,000 has been budgeted for repairs and decorating: nearly $1,400 per unit. The amount seems high, but experience with this 70-year-old building justifies such a high estimate.

When a budget has been prepared for a particular property, enter the figures in the appropriate sections of the Cash Flow Statement. A quick glance at each month's income and expense figures reveals whether a line item entry is above or below the budgeted amount.

When an expense exceeds the budgeted amount it becomes necessary to adjust expenses in another area if the property is to stay within its budget. During a mild winter, for example, the expenditure for heating fuel might fall below the budgeted amount, allowing some excess to be moved to other parts of the budget or to be taken as cash flow. During a severe winter, however, heating fuel might exceed the budgeted amount, making it necessary to cut back on other expenditures.

Operating with a budget provides an opportunity to monitor the performance of the building on a month-by-month basis and to make adjustments as necessary. At the end of the year, the budget for the following year should be developed based upon the present year's experience. When constructing a budget, project not only routine monthly expenditures, but projected capital expenses as well. If the roof will need significant repairs or the boiler is to be replaced, or if the electrical system is to be upgraded, these must all be projected as capital expenditures within the budget.

## Using a Computer

A relatively inexpensive personal computer combined with a good set of property management software can significantly ease the accounting burden. A well-designed software program provides three advantages over manual bookkeeping:

- The ability to manipulate data quickly and accurately.

- The ability to generate records, form letters, notices, etc. quickly and efficiently.

- Less space for keeping records.

Do not expect miracles, however. Using a computer will not reduce the amount of time required to enter data. It takes just as long to type figures into a computer as to write the numbers on a sheet of paper, and operating a computer can be an exasperating task, particularly if you are unfamiliar with the computer or the software. When it comes time to work with the information that has been entered, however, the computer has it all over manual systems, although there are those who would differ with that statement.

### Manipulating Data

Once data has been entered into the computer, it can easily be manipulated. Of course, if you push the wrong buttons, you could also lose all of that wonderful data, so be careful. Rather than totaling the rows and columns by hand in the Cash Flow statement, for example, the computer, if programmed to do so, will compute all such calculations automatically. Monthly expenditures can be compared with budgeted amounts, revealing the percentage over or under budget. Year-to-date figures can reveal the percentage of the annual budgeted amount that has been spent to date. If you wish to know how much money has been spent for utilities so far this year, for example, the computer can provide that number very quickly, a calculation that is both laborious and error-prone when done manually. Likewise, if you wish to compare this year's expenditures for repairs and maintenance with last year's, the information can be generated quickly and effortlessly by computer.

## Saving Space

Keeping records by hand often involves several file drawers, ledger books, etc. Keeping the data in the computer, on the other hand, requires no additional desk space. Be careful, however, to back up all your work on floppy discs or with a special back-up system in the event of computer failure or breakdown.

## Reports

A well-designed software system can generate numerous reports, from the simplest to the most complex. A simple rent roll report, for example, might list each tenant with their monthly base rent, while a more detailed rent roll provides a complex listing of charges and payments for each tenant. A gross potential rent roll reconciles gross potential income with actual cash received and losses due to delinquent rents and concessions and credits. Other reports produce information on individual vacant units, how many days a unit has been vacant, what kinds of units are vacant, when leases are due to expire, scheduled charges for current occupants, as well as general ledger reports and a cash journal. If you manage only one relatively small property, you may find most of the reports that can be generated by the more sophisticated software programs to be unnecessary. On the other hand, if you manage several hundred units you may find such reports to be extremely useful.

## Letters and Notices

Once a data-base has been established (the tenants' names and identifying information have been entered into the computer) tenant letters and notices become easy to produce. A personal letter notifying tenants that the water will be turned off, for example, can be typed, merged with a tenant list, printed and mailed in preaddressed envelopes. Much handier than typing individual letters, much more personal than sending photocopied form letters. The computer may also be programmed to produce lease riders, renewal letters, 5-day notices, and other such documents that require an excessive amount of time when done by hand.

## Choosing a Software Package

If you have decided to use a computer, there are a number of sources for good software. The list of programs in the Appendix includes several promising packages. Consult the Institute of Real Estate Management-produced booklet "Property Management Software Reviews" from *JPM*, 1986-89 and the *Journal of Property Management*, May/June, 1992 (Institute of Real Estate Management, P.O. Box 109025, Chicago, IL 60610-9025) for software reviews. Alternatively, a number of software developers advertise inexpensive property management software in the classified ads in the back of computer magazines. A third alternative is to use a spreadsheet program like Lotus 123 to develop your own accounting program. Unless the spreadsheet is part of a package like MicroSoft Works or Claris Works, however, the program will be limited to accounting only.

# Chapter

# 20

# The Foundation of Effective Property Management Is Effective Property Maintenance

Good maintenance is good business. But maintenance is also the part of property management that is most easily ignored—until something breaks and requires expensive repairs. Of all the items in the operating budget, repairs and maintenance offer the greatest discretionary decision making.

During the heating season, you have no choice but to provide heat. A number of actions can be taken to reduce heating costs, but the fact remains that heating is pretty much a fixed-cost item. The same with electricity, taxes, insurance and mortgage. Peeling paint, however, can be ignored indefinitely—or until the building inspector delivers a citation. A worn-out roof can be patched, rusted gutters can be ignored, a sagging door can be tolerated and crumbling mortar does not usually require immediate attention. For that reason, many property owners and managers put off routine maintenance and scrimp on repairs for years in a misguided attempt to save money.

The truth is, however, where maintenance is concerned, you pay now or you pay later. Skipping over repairs and maintenance in an attempt to save money is, in the popular parlance, "voodoo economics." The dollar you save now may cost two to three dollars in the future, not to mention the hassle of dealing with enraged tenants and the consequence of losing tenants' goodwill. Maintenance and repair costs can be deferred, but not indefinitely. And the unfortunate reality is that the bill to repair the consequences of deferred maintenance is often much higher than the cost of the relatively minor work that could have been performed initially.

The cost of repairs and maintenance should be considered a routine and inevitable expense just like taxes or the electric bill. As a rule of thumb, routine maintenance (primarily cleaning and routine repairs) for a building that is in relatively good condition should cost about 5 percent of the gross income. The cost of repairs (work that is given to outside contractors) will be considerably more than that, but will depend entirely upon the age and condition of the building. If a property generates $75,000 per year, the budget for maintenance should be at least $3,750 per year or just over $300 per month. An older building will need a higher maintenance budget. Repairs should be budgeted at $300 to $750 per unit per year, depending on the size of the units and the condition of the building. The fact is, however, that repairs and maintenance always cost more than anticipated; do not shirk this part of the budget.

## Good Maintenance Is Good Business

Good maintenance is good business for five reasons:

- *Reason #1:* Good tenants. A property that looks well maintained will attract the best tenants, while a property that appears to be poorly maintained will drive away the best tenants: a shabby building discourages high-quality tenants from applying. A poorly maintained building, attracting a less desirable tenant, will consequently suffer greater damage from harder use. The result: higher repair bills and greater management problems.

- *Reason #2:* Ignoring minor problems often leads to major problems. A small leak in the roof, if ignored, may require replastering an entire ceiling. An unpainted window frame will eventually have to be replaced.

- *Reason #3:* Cost control. A well-designed maintenance plan can help keep costs under control. Installing timers on the common area lights, using low energy replacement bulbs, implementing a well-planned timer system on the boiler: all can help reduce operating costs.

- *Reason #4:* Tenant goodwill. Ignoring a small drip in the boiler can lead to a breakdown on a cold Sunday morning when repair costs are double the normal rate and tenants become angry at the inconvenience of being cold in their home on a Sunday morning. The result: extra costs and a loss of goodwill.

- *Reason #5:* Protecting the investment. A well-planned maintenance program helps preserve the value of the property. A properly maintained property holds its value much better than one that has been poorly maintained. A property's value is derived from three important components: the gross income, the condition of the property and the location. Nothing can be done about location, but the quality of maintenance has a direct bearing on both the condition of the building and the gross income (better tenants and lower vacancy rate).

## Preventive Maintenance

For many years the buzzword in property management was preventive maintenance: fixing things before they had the chance to grow into major problems. Buzzwords come and go, but the value of preventive maintenance continues. Preventive maintenance involves three key activities: inspection, anticipation and routine repairs.

- *Inspection:* An effective preventive maintenance program requires making periodic inspections of all the major systems in the building and taking whatever steps are necessary to prevent break-down:

  - *Heating plant:* Inspect the boiler or furnace twice a year, once in the fall just before heating season and once again in the spring at the conclusion of the heating season. Bring in a professional to check the burners, pipes, fittings, ducts, guages and valves—in short, every part of the heating system. Clean everything, paint any rusty pieces and replace any corroded parts. Lubricate the moving parts, seal any leaks and adjust the burner for optimum efficiency. The goal is to maintain the heating plant at optimum efficiency rather than waiting for it to break and then fixing it.

  - *Roof:* Inspect the roof every six months. On a flat roof, check for minor cracks, alligatoring or flashings that are pulling away from walls or pipes. Check the parapet walls for loose or missing mortar, loose tiles and evidence of damage. Look at the chimney for loose mortar, loose brick, flashings that have become unsealed and a missing or broken chimney cover. On a shingle roof, look for broken or missing shingles, flashings in need of repair, broken or rusted gutters, unpainted or rotting sophits and a chimney in need of repair.

    Regardless of which type of roof you have, inspect every inch and patch and repair even the smallest defect. This kind of preventive maintenance preserves the life of the roof and reduces the risk of damaging leaks.

  - *Brick walls:* Check for loose mortar, cracks, broken bricks or any sign of moisture seeping through.

  - *Windows:* Look for peeling paint and broken glazing. Check for looseness, missing or broken panes, missing or broken storm windows and screens.

  - *Doors:* Check for peeling paint, loose hinges, worn-out locks.

Other systems will also need to be inspected periodically, i.e., hallways, stairs, electrical and plumbing systems. Routine inspections are essential to an effective program of preventive maintenance. They also invite procrastination: there's no real urgency to an inspection like there is for other, more demanding aspects of property management. The answer is to remember that good maintenance is good business and schedule your inspections months in advance.

- *Anticipation:* Appliances have a limited useful life. At some point, the cost of repairing a worn-out refrigerator exceeds the cost of replacing it. Similarly, carpet wears out in a predictable fashion and roofs are only good for so long. Keep records on all replacable items in the building: appliances, carpet, heating plant, hot water heater, pumps, etc. Know when they were installed, when they were repaired and their average expected life span. Consider replacing them before they reach the end of their useful existence. Anticipating problems serves two useful purposes: it reduces repair costs and it makes the tenants happy. There's nothing like a new refrigerator, for example, to encourage a top-quality tenant to sign a new two-year lease.

- *Routine Repairs:* As part of a comprehensive preventive maintenance plan, minor repair work around the building must be taken care of quickly and competently by the janitor. A leaky faucet, a broken doorknob, a torn screen or a broken light switch: for these kinds of routine repairs, tenants should contact the janitor directly who, in a timely fashion, solves the problem. An effective property manager, however, does not wait for the tenants to call. Walk the building yourself and urge the janitor to do likewise, looking for minor but necessary repairs. If you see a broken window, have it fixed. If you notice a tenant having trouble with a lock, ask the janitor to take care of it. When you see tenants in the hall, ask if anything needs to be fixed in the apartment. Often, tenants will overlook reporting minor repairs because of the hassle of bringing the janitor into their apartment.

  Rather than ignoring routine repairs, look for them. Watch the water bill decline after replacing washers in five dripping faucets. Notice how much more warmly a tenant smiles at you after you have arranged for the janitor to fix a lock that has been a source of irritation for three months. When it comes time to renew the lease at an increased rate, notice how much more quickly the lease renewal is returned. Preventive maintenance, through the joint activities of inspection, anticipation and routine repairs, looks for problems in their early stage of development and fixes them while they are yet small and easily repaired. An effective program of preventive maintenance, while not cost-free, is designed to save money in the long run by preventing larger and more costly catastrophes and by maintaining tenant goodwill.

## Cost Control

An important part of an effective maintenance program is controlling costs, not only the cost of the work itself but also the cost of utilities.

- *Save money on the work:* Look at each operation within the overall maintenance program: cleaning, landscaping, snow removal, minor repairs, painting, inspection, pest control. Who performs the work? Can the work be accomplished by someone else or in a different manner that will reduce the cost? Can the janitor, for example, do an effective job of pest control, eliminating the need for a professional service?

- *Save money on utilities:* Consider each of following cost-cutting options:

  - Install timers on all common-area lighting, so that bulbs burn only when required. Check the timers periodically as the length of the day varies. Install a timer on the boiler or a programmed thermostat on the furnace to control output and reduce heating costs. Then monitor the controls for the most efficient use. In the Chicago area, the boiler timer settings in Figure 20-1 meet the minimum temperatures re-

### Figure 20–1: Boiler Timer Settings

| BELOW ZERO | | ZERO TO 25 | | 20 TO 35 | |
|---|---|---|---|---|---|
| 4:00 AM | ON | 4:00 AM | ON | 4:30 AM | ON |
| 9:00 AM | OFF | 9:00 AM | OFF | 9:00 AM | OFF |
| 11:30 AM | ON | 11:30 AM | ON | 11:00 AM | ON |
| 1:30 PM | OFF | 1:00 PM | OFF | 12:00 PM | OFF |
| 3:30 PM | ON | 4:00 PM | ON | 4:00 PM | ON |
| 10:00 PM | OFF | 10:00 PM | OFF | 10:00 PM | OFF |
| 12:00 AM | ON | | | | |
| 2:00 AM | OFF | | | | |

| 30 TO 50 | | 40 TO 55 | | 50 TO 60 | |
|---|---|---|---|---|---|
| 5:00 AM | ON | 5:00 AM | ON | 5:00 AM | ON |
| 9:00 AM | OFF | 8:00 AM | OFF | 8:00 AM | OFF |
| 4:00 PM | ON | 6:00 PM | ON | | |
| 10:00 PM | OFF | 9:00 PM | OFF | | |

quired by local ordinances and preserve fuel at the same time.

- Replace high energy incandescent lighting (the most common type of light bulb) with energy efficient fluorescent, metal halide or high pressure sodium vapor lighting.

- Reduce the number of light bulbs. (One 100-watt bulb provides the same light as two 60-watt bulbs with an energy savings of 12 percent.)

- Reduce the size of the light bulbs in use.

- Paint hallways and stairways a light-reflecting white or off-white color.

- Maintain all mechanical equipment in peak condition. A finely tuned, well-running boiler uses far less energy than one that has been neglected.

- Reduce the temperature in the water heater.

- Periodically inspect apartments for leaking faucets, running toilets, loose windows and malfunctioning radiators.

- Hire a professional to tune apartment radiators for maximum efficiency.

- Encourage tenants to report leaky faucets and running toilets.

- Periodically clean refrigerator coils, replace furnace filters and clean light fixtures.

- Insulate hot water pipes and steam pipes to avoid heat loss.

This is only a partial list of the cost cutting measures that can be implemented. For other ideas, contact the utility companies for an energy-saving audit. Most will be happy to tour the building and suggest ways to reduce the cost of utilities.

## Who Does the Work?

### Should You Do the Maintenance Work Yourself?

If you are handy with tools, understand basic plumbing and electricity and have some time available, maintaining the property yourself can save some money. The question is: what is your time worth? If you have only one property, with no plans to purchase another, and you enjoy the work, maintaining the building yourself may be time well spent. If, on the other hand, you are a serious investor wishing to expand your property portfolio, chances are your time should be spent looking for new acquisitions.

## *Outside Contractors*

Some repairs are beyond the purview of the janitor. If a furnace breaks down, if the roof is leaking badly, if a pipe bursts in the basement: these all require outside specialists. As you gain experience with property management, you will learn the best contractors to use: who will provide the best service at the best price. Keep a list of these contractors in a convenient spot so that when a problem develops, you know who to call and how to reach them. Through the years, your list will grow, but you will find that two or three of the names on the list are your most valuable workers. These are the ones who will get up in the middle of the night to take care of a broken pipe, who will give up a Sunday afternoon to fix a cold furnace, who will repair a plaster ceiling and leave no dust and debris behind. In your quest for providing the best possible service to your tenants, these are the workers you will learn to rely on more and more.

## *If You Manage Several Buildings, Should You Employ a Maintenance Crew?*

It is not uncommon for a property management firm with a large portfolio of properties to hire a maintenance crew rather than call in outside contractors. There are some advantages to hiring a crew: you can keep costs under control, you can schedule work, you have some control over the quality of the work and you have individuals available in case of an emergency.

If you are managing enough properties to justify a full-time crew, consider also the disadvantages: employees constitute a fixed expense; outside contractors are a variable expense. Even though the cost of a contractor may be greater for a particular job, you only pay the contractor when there is work to be done. A maintenance crew must be paid whether there is work or not. Taxes and fringe benefits, social security tax, withholding tax, unemployment insurance: the costs of keeping a full-time employee can be high, not to mention the extra bookkeeping. An outside contractor submits an invoice and receives a check. In most circumstances, hiring contractors rather than employees is the most cost-effective plan.

## *Cutting Maintenance Is Bad Business*

The goal of a good property manager is to attract and retain the best tenants. An effective maintenance plan is essential to the accomplishment of that goal. The temptation is always present to cut back on maintenance expenditures, thereby raising profits. Like the lizard eating its own tail, however, reducing necessary maintenance can only temporarily satisfy your appetite for higher profits. At some point, you'll start chewing on something really important.

# Chapter

# 21

# Tenants Are People Too

*"The first day, a guest; the second, a burden; the third, a pest."*
*—Edoudard R. Laboulaye*

**E**very landlord has a favorite tenant story. Most such stories involve fairly typical tenant problems: the chronic complainer, the loud-stereo buff, the loud-mouth, the mural artist. But some stories are truly unique:

The tenant, for example, who became exasperated because the temperature in his apartment never suited him. He thought he could control the heat by wiring a house thermostat to the boiler temperature control. He broke the boiler.

Or the wealthy architect, a resident in a luxury apartment building, who was caught painting obscene graphics on the elevator walls.

Or how about the resident who reported that his upstairs neighbor was spying on him. An inspection of the apartment revealed aluminum foil covering the ceilings. The reason? To thwart the electronic surveillance devices being employed by the neighbor.

No matter how well prepared you may be, no matter how well meaning, property management involves headaches and aggravation.

The best you can hope for is to reduce the aggravation and limit the headaches, but you can never make them go away, no matter how hard you try.

Is property management any different in that respect from any other business that deals with the public? Other than the unique circumstances involved in providing a home, probably not. In fact, most businesses do not enjoy the degree of selectivity available to property managers. As long as the selectivity is not based upon race, creed, color, etc., it is a perfectly suitable tool to use in the property management business.

The wonderful thing about property management is that selectivity can be engineered (through screening prospective tenants), but becomes self-perpetuating (quality tenants, proud of where they live, invite their friends, family and acquaintances to take up residence in the building). Selectivity occurs naturally when the conditions are right—a well-maintained building, a quiet environment, a secure feeling.

And yet, there are the aggravations:

Like the young couple, newly married, with impeccable credentials. Both had professional positions in prominent firms; each had a clean credit history and an excellent rental history. They were in love with each other and with the apartment. The perfect first home for the perfect couple! Perfect, that is, until the wife found the husband fooling around—with another man, no less! She threw him out, only two weeks into the tenancy.

But the story does not end there. Three weeks later the wife, angry and brooding, crashed her car and broke her hip. Unable to work, she lost her job and her income. Unable to pay the rent, she fell behind. Finally, without notice, she moved out, leaving behind a sizable debt.

But what vocation is without aggravation? Those landlords who complain the heartiest about their tenants would probably find little solace in another field. *("Happiness is liking what you do as well as doing what you like." —Dr. Laurence J. Peter.)*

Management of rental property does offer its share of aggravation, yes. Like the tenant who insisted on having her locks changed and refused to give anyone a copy of the new key. Coming home extremely late one night, and a bit tipsy, she locked herself out. The janitor—a yeoman to have responded so even-handedly to her loud ministrations at such a late hour—was helpless to assist, and refused her demands that he break the window or force the door. Complaining bitterly, the tenant checked into a hotel and sent the landlord the bill, which he refused to pay.

But property management also offers more than its share of rewards, good feelings and good times. Like the tenants who chip in each year for a Christmas tree to decorate the patio and then gather to sing carols and toast the season. Or the disabled tenant who, confined to her home, offers to help in any way she can—providing keys to workers, showing apartments, calling when problems arise—because it makes her feel useful. Or . . .

Well, every undertaking offers its share of miseries and joys. The management of rental properties is no different, with one exception. As a property manager, you are in many ways master of your own destiny, able to influence events and manipulate outcomes. Armed with the skills and determined to succeed, you can operate a safe, clean, quiet, well-maintained building that will attract the best tenants. You can nurture a community of residents who will feel comfortable and secure in their homes, and will be grateful. And you can enjoy your work.

*"There is only one success—to be able to spend your life in your own way."*
                                                    *—Christopher Morley*

# Appendix

# Property Management Software Packages

The following is a list of software packages that are presently on the market, arranged from simplest to more complex. Prices range from under $400 to over $3,000, and reflect the degree of sophistication and the number of units that can be managed. In most cases, these software programs are available from your local software dealer. The programs listed here do not exhaust the supply; you might find another program you like better. They are, however, representative of what the market has to offer. All of these packages are suitable for a property manager with a limited number of rental units and uncomplicated leases. For the large property manager, other more sophisticated—and even more expensive—systems are available.

## Propman™ by United Data Systems

This simple, low cost system handles basic rent collection, fees and disbursements, with simple reports for tenants and owners. It prints checks and 1099 tax forms. The program does not include accounting features or entries. Available in three sizes: to handle up to 50 properties, up to 200 properties or up to 1,000 properties.

# Residential Property Manager™ by Real Estate Software Company, Inc.

This system mimics the manual ledger card approach to recordkeeping by visually displaying a "card" on the screen for most transactions. Intended for single family and duplex dwellings only, this program also comes in three sizes: to handle up to 100 units, up to 500 units or up to 1300 units.

# Basic Property Management™ by Yardi Systems, Inc.

A good property and tenant record system, Yardi's basic program handles full accounting plus receivables, payables and scheduled accounts.

# Landlord Plus™

Able to handle 100 properties and 3500 units, Landlord Plus is a complete tenant and property recordkeeping system, including receivables, payables and full accounting services. For a relatively low price, this system offers some of the sophisticated features of more expensive programs, such as multiple tenants per unit, aging of tenant receivables (keeping track of how long a tenant has owed you money) and automatic late fee posting.

# REMS Property Manager™ by Good Software Corporation

REMS Property Manager 500 is a relatively low-priced yet sophisticated property and tenant record keeping system, including such features as square footage, potential rents, insurance expiration dates, multiple tenants and multiple owners. Budget amounts can be matched with actual. A more expensive version can handle up to 2,000 properties.

# Property Management Plus™ by Realty Software Company

This is a basic property and tenant record keeping system, with automatic assessment of late fees, automatic recurring payments and checks printed from multiple invoices per check (one check is written for several invoices from the same vendor).

# Computerized Property Manager™

Able to be connected to an accounting package, this recordkeeping system includes such information as square footage, manager's name, alternate billing address for tenant, and optional module for automatic rent increases.

# Investor Property Manager™ by Realty Automation

This is a combination residential and commercial system that customizes its screen terminology for the type of property (residential, commercial, condos or storage) that is being used. Properties may have variable billing dates and grace periods, with multiple owners or tenants per unit. Other features include automatic late fees, recurring or scheduled expense payments and a full accounting module.

# Prime-Avenue™

Prime-Avenue provides comprehensive tenant management and a full accounting system. Designed for professional management companies, the system maintains a complete file of information about tenants, owners and units, and includes modules for receivables, payables, maintenance records and management fee calculator. It can store 2 years of data.

# Comtronic Property Manager (CPM)™ by Comtronic Systems, Inc.

A bit more expensive than the others in the list, CPM also offers a few more features, like full accounting, a tenant communications package that includes letters,notices, statements and an internal text processor, and a maintenance package that includes work order monitoring and a preventive maintenance orientation.

# Index

# E

Earnest money deposit, 69
Electrical fixtures/outlets, 44, 45, 103
Elevator, 95, 195
Employees, 2, 3, 4, 103, 138-156, 193
Employer, 68
Employment, 63, 73
  *see* Self, Un
  type, 9, 13, 14, 17
  verification, 71, 72
Escrow account, 174, 177
Eviction, 71, 119, 121, 123, 149, 159, 163
  process, 125-126
Expiration, 127, 134
  *see* Five, Lease

# F

Family status, 8, 11, 15
Field, Marshall, 1, 2
Final inspection, 94
Five-day notice, 119-125, 163
  expiration, 119, 123-125
Floors, 9, 26, 34, 44, 45

# G

Gangs, 15
Garage, 94, 97
  rent, 170
  rider, 79, 84
Garbage, 95
Grace period, 110

# H

Hallways, 47, 191
Heating plant, 188, 189
High-rise, 9
Housing stock, 8, 11, 15

# I

Identification
  *see* Picture
  driver's license number, 68
  Social Security number, 68
Incentives, 4
Income, 9, 13, 14, 17, 63, 69, 73-74, 117, 172, 178, 179, 186, 187
  *see* Investment
  alternative sources, 69, 73, 74
  amount, 73-74
  verification, 69, 73
Inquiry call, 49-53
Inspection, 106, 187-188, 190
  *see* Final
Insurance, 174, 185, 193
Interest, 174
Investment income, 69, 73
Invoice(s), 169

# J

Janitor, 95, 102, 104, 105, 138, 139-144, 146, 153, 169, 177, 189, 190
  characteristics, 139
  contract, 141
  duties, 140

# About the Author

In a field dominated by male professionals, Susan Underhill (Manisco) has used her arsenal of "street smart" skills to establish herself as a formidable expert in real estate investing, gaining the respect and admiration of her male counterparts along the way. And her success story is even more amazing given the fact that she is entirely self taught.

Underhill grew up in Chicago with a keen understanding of the neighborhoods and the people who live there. She began her real estate career in 1975 with a small savings account accumulated—with great effort—from her modest earnings as a teacher. Since then she has used her grasp of the real estate markets to parlay that hard-earned stake into a lucrative real estate business.

As a member of various community and professional organizations, Underhill works with local and industry leaders to maintain high standards for herself and other property owners in the neighborhoods. While building her personal real estate empire, Underhill also developed a successful career as a special educator. Having now "retired" from teaching to pursue real estate interests full time, her masters degree and 16 years as a professional educator have proven an asset in her ability to teach her techniques to others.

While it has been said that real estate investing is not for everyone, Underhill has proven, by example, that the right skills—all of which can be learned through persistence and effort—can help virtually anyone achieve success.

## About the Publisher

PROBUS PUBLISHING COMPANY

Probus Publishing Company fills the informational needs of today's business professional by publishing authoritative, quality books on timely and relevant topics, including:

- Investing
- Futures/Options Trading
- Banking
- Finance
- Marketing and Sales
- Manufacturing and Project Management
- Personal Finance, Real Estate, Insurance and Estate Planning
- Entrepreneurship
- Management

Probus books are available at quantity discounts when purchased for business, educational or sales promotional use. For more information, please call the Director, Corporate/Institutional Sales at 1-800-PROBUS-1, or write:

Director, Corporate/Institutional Sales
Probus Publishing Company
1925 N. Clybourn Avenue
Chicago, Illinois 60614
FAX (312) 868-6250